QUAGLINO'S

THE COOKBOOK

RICHARD WHITTINGTON

RECIPES BY MARTIN WEBB

First published in 1995 by Conran Octopus Limited,
37 Shelton Street, London WC2H 9HN

Reprinted 1995 (twice), 1996, 1997

First published in the USA in 1996 by
The Overlook Press

ISBN 1 85029 791 6

USA Edition ISBN 0 87951 678 X

Cataloguing in Publication Data: a catalogue record for
this book is available from the British Library.

Commissioning Editor Louise Simpson
Art Director Helen Lewis
Design Helen Lewis and Liz Hallam
Production Jill Macey
Picture Research Jessica Walton
Editorial Assistant Helen Green
Copyeditor Lewis Esson
Indexer Hilary Bird

Picture Acknowledgements:
Page 6 courtesy of Express Newspapers plc
Quaglino's Story, pages 14–17 Marcus Harrison
Quaglino's Reborn, pages 20–37 David Brittain
Day in the Life of... Robert Mort
Food photography James Murphy
Food for Photography Quaglino's

Both metric and imperial quantities are given in the
recipes in this book. Use either all metric or all imperial.

Colour separations by Chroma Graphics, Singapore
Printed in Hong Kong, produced by Mandarin Offset

Page 1: Antipasti of soft polenta, olives & baby leeks
Page 2: Carpaccio of beef with rocket & parmesan
Above: The writer and the chef: Richard Whittington and
Martin Webb

CONTENTS

The restaurant is a glittering and airy room that stretches away from and behind the stairs of the mezzanine floor. By mid-evening, when service is at its peak, the collective energy of the diners is tangible.

The design of a restaurant is the most testing job that any designer can get involved with. You have to have a vision, but also the understanding of how to take that vision and put it in a wholly practical context. The choice of every item involves time, knowledge and research. And it is vital you don't let the physical perfection slide, because it is inextricably linked to the quality of the food. If either slips it brings the other down. If the glasses are not polished or the service gets sloppy then you have lost it.

The style of a restaurant that you design will determine how it wears with time. At Quag's there is nothing which will change significantly, though there will come a patina of maturity. It is going to look much the same in ten years as it did after ten days. When you have a design strategy it includes repainting and refitting, because they can often be cheaper options than cleaning. All of these practical issues are by definition also business issues. A restaurateur must be professional. Enthusiasm and energy alone are not enough, which is why 95 per cent of new restaurants fail within three years. But a profit focus and getting costs controlled is not enough either. Accounting skills don't give a restaurant a heart or a unique identity. You have to love and understand what restaurants can deliver to the customer before you can make them an enduring success.

I get a genuine thrill every time I go to Quag's. There's a buzz of excitement that I find irresistible and, judging from the bookings, it's a sensation shared by many others. This book is a handsome testimony to the architects, designers and craftsmen I worked with, to the culinary brilliance of Martin Webb and the expertise of Richard Whittington, and to the tireless enthusiasm of Joel Kissin. Like Quaglino's, the restaurant, Quaglino's: The Cookbook *is exuberant, theatrical and justifiably proud of its food.*

Terence Conran.

QUAGLINO'S STORY

London high society in the 1920s emerged for the first time from private houses to play in public – or at least in hotels, clubs and restaurants – and after the horrors of the First World War it did so with a defiant exuberance. This was the era of the cocktail, and nights were for dancing until dawn. The dress was indisputably black tie; life was high for hedonists and the decadence was neatly encapsulated by the songs of Cole Porter such as 'I get no kicks from champagne'.

Despite high society's relaxed attitudes, a legal requirement of the day stipulated that in clubs alcohol could only be served with food, which meant that any inedible rubbish would do, simply for compliance; something that scarcely encouraged a culture of *haute cuisine*. As the decade drew to a close and the manic atmosphere calmed a little, however, even the younger socialites started to notice what they were eating. The party went on, but now it was attended by people who dined as well as danced.

The most famous restaurant of the period was Sovrani's in Jermyn Street, its popularity largely due to the head waiter Giovanni Quaglino, an ambitious Italian from Piedmont whose early career had been meteoric in the smartest hotels of the Côte d'Azur and distinguished by a spell as the maître d'hôtel of the Martinez in Cannes at the precocious age of seventeen. John Quaglino – as he became known in London – and Sovrani had become friends while working together at the Savoy and had left to set up Sovrani's, the restaurant, with John playing the front-of-house role to Sovrani's general manager. Their joint popularity brought many of the Savoy's customers with them and Sovrani's soon became the smartest place to dine. It did not last long, for their relationship crumbled when Sovrani made a play for John's wife. Furious at this personal betrayal, John decided to quit and set up in opposition, a move supported by Lady Furness, a very influential figure in café society at that time.

John knew that the restaurant just around the corner in the basement of the St James's Palace Hotel (later the Hotel Meurice) was losing money, and suggested to the

Quaglino's has always made a point of creating special menus for very special occasions, and some of the dishes listed on this Derby Day in 1933 would not be out of place today – although the mixing of French and English might now be thought a touch tongue in cheek.

Chez Quaglino

DERBY NIGHT
GALA
DINNER

31st Ma
1933

Menu

Caviar de Sterlet aux Brioches

-

Rossolnick Livonienne

-

Délice de Sole Ernest

-

Suprême de Volaille Derby
Pommes Magda
Velouté de Petit Pois de
Jersey

-

Asperges d'Evesham
Vinaigrette

-

Fraises Recamiers
Biscuits Glacés
Sigurd
Mignardises

AT MIDNIGHT

JEAN ADRIENNE

5 TH. **BIRTHDAY**

CHEZ QUAGLINO

management that he take it over and run it under his name. This was an era when the maître d'hôtel and not the chef was the crowd-puller and Quaglino obviously had star quality that, with the patronage of Lady Furness, made a potent commercial combination. A deal was soon struck and Quaglino's Restaurant opened in Bury Street in 1929. It was a palpable hit from day one and quite the most fashionable place to be and be seen throughout the 1930s.

Quaglino's was, by all accounts, an outstanding success for a variety of reasons. There was the personality of Quaglino himself, described by Lord Forte in his autobiography as 'a short plump man, immaculately turned out with an attractive frog-like face'. His younger brother Ernest, the head waiter, was younger, taller and very good-looking. Both applied their charm to maximum effect, but it was John who became known as the perfect greeter. It was said that no female visitor could fail to be impressed by the gracious way in which he would present her with a flower as if she was the only person ever to have been so favoured. The epitome of the suave host, he flattered his regulars by name but was neither overly familiar nor obsequious, contriving that fine line between due deference and professional courtesy that proved irresistible. 'How marvellous to see you,' he would say as if he really meant it. A favourite line as he seated somebody was: 'Why don't you sit over there? You know you are my best customer. I do not let anyone else have this table. Even if the Queen came in, she would have to sit somewhere else.'

And even if Queen Mary did not, other royals did. Lord Forte recalled an occasion when the clientele included the Prince of Wales, King Alfonso of Spain and King Carol of Rumania. He wrote 'Only John Quaglino could have managed that combination. Royalty, even minor royalty, require great skill to handle correctly. They must be treated with respect but without fuss.' However, royalty had no special privileges. According to Forte, 'every guest was made to feel that he was the only person who mattered. That was the atmosphere he established and you left his restaurant feeling on top of the world.'

Charm alone would not have made Quaglino's – the success of which soon eclipsed Sovrani's, which was forced to close. So John had his revenge and saw all the customers he had served there decamp to Bury Street. The process was helped by the Prince of Wales, who adopted it as his favourite West End haunt. The Prince, who was to return in the 1950s as the Duke of Windsor, did not like dressing for dinner – an absolute requirement at Quaglino's. John made a private dining room for his exclusive use that meant he could dress as he wished. It was a place where he could entertain without being seen – something that was known about without being openly discussed, and which gave the restaurant even greater social cachet than if his visits had been conducted in a blaze of publicity, which would have been thought common. His regular nights there also meant that journalists had to be careful about what they wrote, important for business in an age where gossip had plenty of meat on which to feed.

Barbara Cartland, a Quag's regular before the war, remembers John as the soul of tact and discretion. 'In those days a good maître d'hôtel knew all the scandal and the gossip. It would have been disastrous to put a recently divorced couple at adjacent tables, or a budding romance next to a noisy party. He knew when love was blooming and he also sensed very perceptively when it was waning. A special dish, a glass of brandy, or a liqueur on the house would often salvage a marriage drifting near the rocks.'

And, of course, there was the food. At a time when it was considered bad manners to discuss what one ate, Quaglino's food was noticed and talked about. He introduced hot hors d'oeuvres and a menu which – in today's terms – we have learned to call eclectic. Here were culinary innovations aplenty. Typically its menus were in French and not without their amusing moments, offering such geographical non-sequiturs as Poussins de Surrey Sicilienne and Petits Pois de Kent. Multicultural influences were there 60 years before our current generation of chefs 'invented' them: braised pheasant with celery might be served with a Japanese salad, while you could find quiche Lorraine and chicken curry juxtaposed on the same *prix fixe* lunch with smoked salmon and pears poached in red wine.

The menus were always beautifully balanced. Consider an autumn dinner of native oysters, consommé with Parmesan biscuits, a crab soufflé, noisettes of milk-fed lamb with buttered spinach and a simple dessert of pineapple or peaches. It sounds as tempting today as it must have done then. A summer supper might have started with Charentais melon followed by chilled Borscht before langoustines in a Bordelaise sauce, then an Aylesbury duck breast sliced and served pink and cold with a grapefruit salad. Dessert was an iced soufflé with raspberries and peaches. One imagines there were few complaints that night.

The outbreak of war brought the curtain down temporarily on Quaglino's. As Italian nationals, John and Ernest decided to return to their homeland rather than be interned on the Isle of Man. Ironically, they were locked up in Italy instead for expressing anti-fascist views – something which one would have expected to ease their return to Britain after the war, but not so. Their application for permanent residence was rejected and it was only with the greatest difficulty that John obtained temporary visitor's visas that allowed him to return from time to time to monitor his business, which in his absence was understandably fading fast. Forte, by now a personal friend, eventually got to see Sir Frank Newsam, then Permanent Secretary at the Home

Quag's fifth birthday, in 1934, was worth celebrating. The restaurant was at the height of its popularity and packed with regulars every night. Memories of the last war had eased with time, while few considered the grim possibility that the next was just around the corner. It was a night when the champagne never stopped and the dancing went on until dawn.

Sprawling on the stairs would have been improper in the 1930s, but in the 1950s things were starting to relax with rock 'n' roll, Teddy boys, juke boxes and coffee bars. Street credibility was a drape suit; and girls' skirts swirled around the knee, plumped with multi-layered petticoats. At Quaglino's the dress remained determinedly black tie (left and far left), although the behaviour, by all accounts, grew more rowdy as the decade drew to a close.

Office, to plead the brothers' case and did so successfully. John and Ernest were allowed to return to Quaglino's, which again in the 1950s returned to centre-stage as one of the smartest places in town.

Marcus Harrison, who came to England from Australia in 1952, remembers Quaglino's well from his nights there as its official photographer. He describes it as being like an old English drawing room in a rather grand house. 'Everything was mixed up and slightly shabby as though, like the aristocrats it mainly served, it did not need to define itself socially. It had the confidence of knowing who it was and where it was. It did not need to aspire or pretend. In 1953 it had this charming air of being an extension of someone's home and at the same time of being indisputably a restaurant.

Every table had lit candles with little pink shades, which suffused the room with a pretty light but had to be kept serviced by the waiters as they burned down.

The room was long, with banquettes running round its perimeter and tables of varying sizes. Above them was a mock baroque frieze, loosely inspired by Watteau. When busy, tables for two were set up around the circular sprung dance floor in the middle. The colour scheme was mostly a faded apricot pink with detail picked out in white, with a pelmet from which ruched curtains were suspended at either side. The music and dancing were very important, with a number of top entertainers of the day appearing on a regular basis. The star attraction was undoubtedly velvet-voiced Hutch, who had come to London from Grenada in

The Duke of Windsor hated wearing a dinner jacket, but in public he bowed to convention. Perhaps this explains the uncharacteristically solemn faces.

1927, and among whose many society conquests gossip includes Lady Mountbatten. He invariably sang Cole Porter to requests from the floor: 'It was just one of those things', 'Night and day' and, appropriately enough in a late-night atmosphere where the possibility of imminent sex gave the dancing a discernible frisson, 'Let's do it'. This never failed to bring the house down and encores were always demanded.

Despite the importance of the entertainment, food remained central to the mix and was served up with a great deal of éclat. There was always a lot of flambé work at the table and the cold hors d'oeuvres were presented on a great multi-tiered trolley. The food was good but not exceptional – certainly good enough, however, in a situation where cocktails, dancing and having fun were the primary order of the day. Hutch

wore tails, the head waiter wore a white dinner jacket, the other waiters wore black. Photographs of some of the customers looking mightily dishevelled as the night wore on suggest that the aphorism, 'some men in dinner jackets look like waiters while others are less fortunate' could well have been coined here.

Quaglino's went on through the 1960s, but the world was changing and gradually, as the reality of John's magic receded with the passage of time and the black-tie formula dissipated, it slid sadly into decay. The ownership had passed from the Quaglino brothers first to Queen Anne's Hotel & Property Ltd and then, in 1964, to Trusthouse Forte, who were never to make a go of it – it finally closing in 1977. For 20 years Quaglino's ceased to exist save in the memories of its past denizens and as a title on a piece of paper.

Her Majesty the Queen arrives to dine at Quaglino's on a rainy night in 1956 as The Duke of Edinburgh waits with the doormen.

QUAGLINO'S REBORN

At night-time, the entrance to Quag's in Bury Street has a welcoming glow (above, left).

Flowers play an important part in the ambient mix, making colourful statements against muted backgrounds (above, right).

Looking back from the bar, the area is flooded with natural light. The bas-relief by Dhruva Mistry is lit by recessed halogen spotlights (far right).

Arrive early at Quaglino's if you can, for to experience this great room briefly devoid of customers is to enjoy the restaurant at its most deliciously theatrical. The stage is set: a glittering, glamorous affair of light and space. You enter through a reception area of warm honeyed stone that leads you down a first sweeping staircase into the bar area. This is on a mezzanine platform that projects into the room and connects to the main floor below by another imposing flight of marble stairs, which are flanked by gleaming bronze handrails incorporating the shining 'Q' motif.

Scan round the room as you look down from the bar: the central flower displays are pure spectacle, great bursts of colour in a high-ceilinged room that has otherwise pointedly eschewed flamboyance. All is brightly lit by the central pale-blue artificial 'skylight' that actually changes as the day goes on in a conscious

simulation of the natural light outside. On your left, angled mirrors on the wall reflect the tables, serried ranks of white linen contrasting with the warm red of the middle tables that run with banquettes the length of the room. The banquettes create a central divide, making two parallel service areas of the floor space, cut through with walkways. Track down the room and close on the crustacea altar, with its cascades of shellfish and mounds of glittering ice. To the right, tantalising glimpses of the kitchen and service areas, backdrop visuals that remind you the restaurant is as much off-stage as on. Here nothing happens by chance and functionality underpins everything.

Quaglino's, in the moments before service, has a frisson of excitement, a palpable ripple of nervous anticipation. For the staff it is the breathless moment of calm before the inexorable onset of high-pressure

QUAGLINO'S
REBORN

activity. The finishing touches are put to the room: an elegant black-suited manager pauses to wipe at an almost-invisible mark on one of the columns; a striking girl with short-cropped hair and a striped jacket moves a chair a few inches, then repositions a wine glass; behind a bar, white-jacketed staff move in a fluid dance. Slowly the tables start to fill. As people begin to arrive, orders are placed and the operation notches into first gear. Out of the corner of your eye there is constant movement, a flicker of activity. The kitchen begins the service and trays of food are brought out, held high by the blue-jacketed runners as they swing smoothly across the room to the waiter stations. The noise lifts a level and the restaurant pot heats from a tremble to a simmer. The rising sound occasionally impinges on

your consciousness as the volume is cranked upwards until it peaks, becoming an integral part of the volatile mix which is Quaglino's flat out, a high-energy event at a rolling boil. It is always an intense experience.

You focus on the people with you at the table, leaning in closer to catch the words as they are tossed back and forth. Laughter is always present, erupting here, effervescing there. There is a sense of occasion. And the food keeps coming. How does the kitchen do it, you wonder, because every dish is good.

When you look away to other tables, you will see people giving each other forkfuls from their plates to taste. Chips arrive in big, deep bowls to be seized by wayward fingers that plunge in from every direction; a *plateau de fruits de mer* is assembled for a table of six

Attention is paid to even the smallest details; here, brass rivets on the acid-etched zinc of the pillars in the bar (above left).

The bar offers its own menu for those who want to eat informally, and tables provide a grandstand view of the activity below. The unusual maple and leather chairs were created by Sean Sutcliffe of Benchmark (above, centre).

– a towering, three-tiered pyramid of sea freshness; the flame rotisseries turn heavily peppered rib-eyes of beef and great tranches of marinated lamb; and drink is consumed joyously because people come here in a generous spirit. They are sharing an occasion, not simply a meal.

When you eat at Quaglino's you inevitably join a larger party. You come here to be with your friends, but then unconsciously play a part in a bigger picture. Other people do not intrude, but their collective energy is tangible. It is an infectious high and those who arrive looking glum visibly brighten within minutes of being seated. It would be difficult not to. This is the main event in town and it happens seven days a week.

Any day in the life of Quaglino's is a fascinating story, involving more than 200 staff in a carefully structured service that encompasses every aspect of the restaurant business on a scale that is quite staggering. The logistics of the operation are extraordinary – from the heating, cooling, ventilating and refrigerating systems that control every aspect of the environment to the high-energy demands of the kitchen and the more prosaic, but equally important, support services like cleaning. The volume and value of produce and wines alone, and the ordering processes that ensure their supply all year round, make for entertaining reading. Each week, among other things, an average 36kg of fresh foie gras, 240kg of live crab, 1.5 tonnes of potatoes for frites and 500kg of potatoes for mashing, 1,000

The bar's grand piano helps keep Quaglino's tradition of live music shining, with a pianist playing nightly and a jazz trio swinging into the early hours on Fridays and Saturdays (above, right).

Each service is staffed by a manager, two first head waiters, ten head waiters, ten chefs de rang, 12 runners, three barmen, three bar waiters and one cashier. There are four receptionists, two cloakroom attendants, a shop assistant, a doorman, three telephonists and a lavatory attendant. All wear uniforms designed by Jasper Conran, which clearly identify the serving hierarchy. The managers and chief head waiters wear plain suits, waiters have striped jackets and black trousers, runners dark blue jackets, while bartenders wear white. Chefs wear white jackets and checked trousers, kitchen porters dark blue nylon jackets and trousers. The doorman wears a classic uniform in grey with a peaked cap, and in the evening there is a cigarette girl in a deliberately sexy, short, flared dress and high heels – obviously tongue in cheek, but a light-hearted touch that has displeased some critics. The kitchen has 82 people including porters, while the private dining room that seats 40 on the mezzanine floor has its own staff of three – a working team of more than 100 for each shift. A specially commissioned computer reservations system handles 1,200 telephone calls a day and ensures that capacity is maintained with maximum efficiency. It is typical of the strategic planning that characterizes operational management here, as central to the Quaglino's style as the broad vision which allowed its creation and the even bolder investment of almost £3 million that made it possible. And it all started with a hole in the ground and an extraordinary vision shared by Sir Terence Conran and Joel Kissin, Chairman and Managing Director respectively of Conran Restaurants.

Terence Conran, famous as the founder of Habitat, had taken his first tentative steps as a restaurateur 40 years ago when he embraced the idea of good food for a wider public and introduced cheap and cheerful Soup Kitchens in several locations. These were followed, in 1956, by The Orrery, a rather more serious restaurant; he then designed The Chanterelle in South Kensington. In 1971 he opened The Neal Street Restaurant in Covent Garden, an elegant and mould-breaking venture that encapsulated both his love of good simple food and his belief that design must be functional if it is

The restaurant is dominated by the massive 'skylight' that runs down the middle of the room (above and far right). The computer-controlled lighting system is programmed to reflect the change in natural light through the course of the day, gradually fading to a deep blue during the night.

lettuces, 200kg of butter, 105kg of sea bream, 210kg of salmon, 120kg of live lobsters, 84kg of scallops, 240kg of entrecôte steaks, 140kg of cod, 8,500 rolls, 2,000 lemons, 170 litres of olive oil, 525 litres of cream, 105kg of watercress, 105kg of freshwater crayfish, 115kg of flat-leaf parsley and 5,000 live oysters are consumed. The food is washed down with 500 bottles of champagne and 4,620 bottles of wine a week. Including mineral water, more than 360,000 empty bottles are recycled a year – as is all paper and wood. Laundry costs £6,000 per month for linen, which includes 10,000 table napkins a week. Overnight restaurant cleaning services cost a further £16,500 each month, while £1,000 a week is spent on flowers.

QUAGLINO'S REBORN

to be effective. David Hockney designed the menu, the works of now-famous British painters adorned the walls, and the downstairs bar was a joyous experience with pistachios on the table and perfect Bloody Marys and Martinis for the discerning drinker – a rarity then as now. In 1987, with Paul Hamlyn and Simon Hopkinson, he opened Bibendum in the beautiful Michelin Building at Brompton Cross.

Conran then fell in love with the old spice grinders' riverside site at Butlers Wharf by Tower Bridge, and in 1989 set up the Design Museum there, which incorporated the 86-seat Blue Print Café on its mezzanine level. Conran had found Joel Kissin at the same time as he discovered Simon Hopkinson, when the former was managing Hilaire in Old Brompton Road and the latter was making his name as its chef – and whose particular enthusiasm for redefining classic French bourgeois cooking was shared by Conran. He saw them as the perfect partnership to set up and run Bibendum, and head-hunted them as a team. Kissin, then in his early thirties, rapidly demonstrated the kind of restaurant management expertise that has since taken him to the top of his profession. Today he is one of the most influential restaurateurs in Britain, running five of London's most successful restaurants, with a total seating capacity of 1,239, and with a sixth, the 700-seater Mezzo in Wardour Street, Soho, newly opened in the autumn of 1995. He is a charming, quietly spoken New Zealander who generally shuns publicity, but is known as a tough negotiator and a demanding employer.

The Quaglino's story really begins in 1991 while both men are wholly focused on the lease for Le Pont de La Tour, a restaurant capable of seating 287, which has been in negotiation for months. It is eventually signed with Butlers Wharf Ltd., but Midland Bank refuses to ratify the document because of fiscal uncertainty and the ugliness of recession which is now hurting everybody. It would be difficult to choose a more difficult time to finance grandiose restaurant schemes and, without the bank's support, administrative receivership is inevitable. When it happens, Kissin

shrugs his shoulders like the fighter he is and starts to renegotiate the lease with the receivers, now on behalf of Conran personally. As January slips into February he sits alone in his office, staring glumly at a £3,500 bill for a telephone system in Butlers Wharf and cursing himself for being over-ambitious. His mood is as grey as the Thames sliding by outside the window and, without a secretary, he is opening the mail himself. Among the other bills, sales flyers, and the usual pile of job applications, is information about a restaurant site in St James's. It is as centrally located as it could possibly be – on the east side of Bury Street, a few yards south of its junction with Jermyn Street and two minutes walk from Piccadilly – and its 10,000 square feet of space is being offered by the landlords, Forte, on a 99-year lease.

'It is odd to think I was agonizing about how I would justify the cost of the telephone system if everything went down the tubes. Now it is used by Pont, The Butlers Wharf Chop-house and Cantina del Ponte, handling thousands of calls a week and we could not manage without it; but at the time it was looking like I had been grossly over-optimistic. Then, through the post came information about Quaglino's – which seemed vast at the time. They were asking a huge amount of money, but the location was terrific so I went and had a look at it and found myself walking into this vast empty shell without even any lights, so I stumbled round peering at it with a torch. Even so I was struck immediately by the potential. I spoke to Terence and said how brilliant I thought it was, though I imagined that would be the end of it.'

In fact it was the beginning, as Conran recalls. 'Although I was in the final throes of designing Le Pont de la Tour, I decided to go and look at the site. The moment I saw it I felt it could be what I had always dreamed possible in London, a restaurant on a grand scale, like La Coupole in Paris, with that uniquely buzzy French quality.' The only vestiges left of the old Quag's were the eight huge columns marching down the length of this dark cavern. The scale took his breath away and, as he looked upwards, he saw enough

height to put in a mezzanine floor that gave a further 5,000 square feet and radically changed the commercial value of the property. His heart was in it from that moment. The more he thought about the commercial opportunity, the more convinced he became and within days he had instructed his managing director to start negotiating for the site.

Kissin had no experience of doing so on such a large scale and was at the same time still arguing backwards and forwards with the administrative receivers over Le Pont. 'Suddenly both deals started to get really hot. I asked Terence which should we prioritize? Le Pont was the obvious choice because it was already designed and we were really in a situation where all we needed to do was push the button to get things rolling very quickly. On the other hand, Quaglino's was a more obvious commercial decision. Terence did not

hesitate. "We'll do them both", he said. I don't think I would have had the chutzpah to do two huge projects, but he had no doubts.'

The Quaglino's name meant little to Kissin, but for Conran, who had been there in the 1960s, it had very positive associations and he was adamant that it was key to the deal. Kissin was soon equally committed to the title, but was worried that while all the papers that had gone backwards and forwards had Quaglino's written at the top, there was no confirmed legal right to use the name. 'We had always presumed it would be ours, but suddenly I had a queasy feeling that this was not a safe assumption. Ivor Collins, our solicitor, raised the matter casually at one of the finalizing meetings. We were told no, in a way that left us in no doubt. Lord Forte was personally very fond of the name, believed it to be a valuable property, and had no intention of

Glimpses of the kitchen can be seen by customers, a deliberate design strategy which does not bring the working reality intrusively to the table, but reminds us that a restaurant is an environment where delivery requires a seamless integration between front and back of house (above).

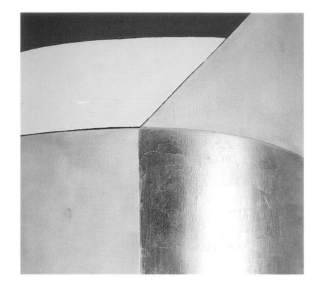

parting with it.' It was time for another piece of brinkmanship. He insisted the name came with the property or the deal was off. After a few days agonizing, they capitulated and it was all systems go again.

For the outsider, the precise process of how a great restaurant emerges from a hole in the ground is a mystery, but by this time Conran, Kissin and their project designer Keith Hobbs had a lot of experience. Conran did the initial drawings in the space of one weekend in the country. 'As the ideas took shape on paper I knew we had a success in the making. It had a good feeling right from day one, and there was a buzz about the project long before we finished the build.' Keith Hobbs' role was then crucial, dealing with the hard practical issues and turning the design outlines into working architectural drawings. As he explained, 'You need to have a vision, but you also must start with the mundane realities, and in a restaurant like Quag's which is mostly below ground level, that means beginning with how people escape in the event of fire, with air in and heat out, with goods inwards and rubbish outwards. Drainage was a major problem. Such logistical issues dominate early thinking and

planning long before you think about what it's going to look like.' Much time was spent agonizing over disabled access which to this day remains via the kitchen lift. It simply proved impossible to put in a lift at the main street entrance.

Before the site opportunity arose in Bury Street, Conran had some discussions with Monsieur Boucher of the Flo Group in Paris about the idea of doing a big Parisian-style brasserie in London. Boucher had long seen London as a logical target for expansion and was looking for a British partner, but it rapidly transpired that this would not be Conran. 'He said there was only one way to do this and it was in the classic French style of La Coupole, with its fake *fin de siècle* appearance, which I disagreed with profoundly. I was not in the business of doing a reproduction anything and we decided to go our own way. I saw an opportunity for something modern with modern food; not a brasserie, but a restaurant on a grand scale. That being said, the inspiration was the original Alsatian brasserie and some of the food you will always get at Quag's includes chips, steaks, oysters and plain grilled fish, the sort of dishes that people who eat out regularly adore. If there

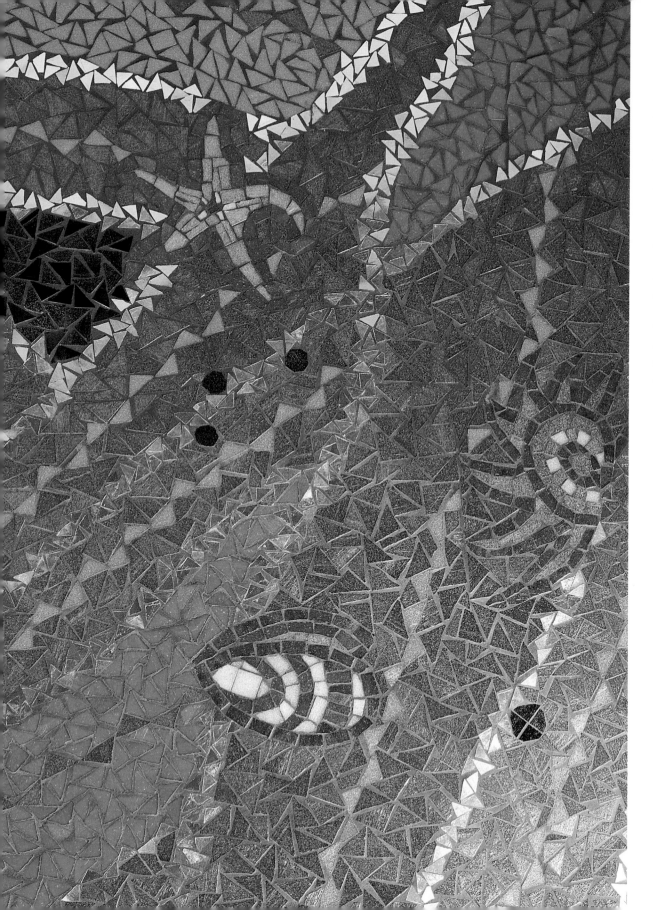

A detail from Catherine Keraly's painted column, bringing further colour to the restaurant (far left, left).

The best and freshest shellfish smell only of the sea. They are held briefly on great beds of crushed ice at the crustacea bar, a splendid cascade of natural colours (far left, right).

The mosaic tiling of the crustacea display was created by Tessa Hunkin and Emma Biggs (left).

is a symbol of everything good about brasseries then for me it is the waiter coming out with the tray held high, which represents the essential triumvirate of food, service and systems.'

People doubted Conran's ability to deliver good food either at Le Pont de la Tour or Quag's, saying they were too big. In a sense, the critics were only reflecting Conran and Kissin's own concerns, because both restaurants were to develop away from their original conceptions of cheap food and fast turnover. Kissin points out that guesswork did not come into it. 'Quaglino's was based on intensive research which always means eating in other people's restaurants, but I felt jaded and in need of exposure to the source so I went off to Paris to check out the big brasseries and in particular those of the Flo Group where I was generously given unlimited access behind the scenes.'

He ate lunch and dinner for seven days, jotting notes as he did so on everything from how the waiters were organized to the cutlery, glasses and the kitchen equipment. He took hundreds of pictures and also visited the factory outside Paris where a lot of the large-scale kitchen cooking equipment is made. He measured the tables and plates, looked at the systems, absorbed the fine detail. 'It was exhausting, but I returned to London oddly refreshed and with some clear ideas starting to gel. I can honestly say that I did not copy so much as take on board the spirit of those places. I got to understand their synergy and to feel their vibrancy, their energy.'

On his return he discussed his trip with Conran and Hobbs and then the work started in earnest. 'Terence has central themes which drive us forward. At Quag's these included the skylight, the central banquettes with the huge flower arrangements dominating the room and dividing it into two, and the visual feature of the crustacea display with its service point at the far end of the room. He also wanted the mezzanine floor and bar looking down on the restaurant floor. Keith took these outlines and key features and pulled everything together. We all three worked together, bounced ideas off one another, argued and disagreed before finally agreeing. The process got more and more detailed as we went along and the issue of the trays was a case in point. Terence hates anything made of plastic or rubber and wanted beautiful silver trays. Of course they look nicer and if we had them you'd get all these lovely reflections, but the waiters and runners would not be able to carry them high because of the weight, and you would have problems because of the slippery surface. I also wanted them large enough so everything could be brought out from the kitchen in one go. Finally we agreed on plain black compound trays with a rubberized surface.'

Everything in the end has to be resolved in this way. Kissin, for example, was determined that the waiters' stations would be tidy yet capable of handling the laundry from within each station. Cutlery is kept out of the way in a designed recess, while key stations have a

The lavatories are every bit as glamorous as the rest of Quag's. In the Ladies (far left), spotlessly clean polished-steel handbasins are set into granite; the single, touch-sensor tap and soap dispenser are a typical blend of the functional and the aesthetic. In the Gents (left), a gently angled slab of russet marble forms a washbasin running the length of the alcove.

Banquettes run down the middle of the restaurant. Above them, generously filled vases punctuate the steel luggage racks (right).

The private dining room overlooks the restaurant but is completely separate from it. Accessed from the bar area and seating up to 40 people, it has been a success story in its own right, operating at maximum capacity all year round (far right).

QUAGLINO'S REBORN

telephone that allows them to communicate directly with the chefs so the waiters never need to go into the kitchen. That is the runners' job. Attention to detail is absolute: from the aluminium ashtray designed by Terence and Sebastian Conran that doubles – when coated black – as a salt and pepper holder, to the silver sugar bowl which also forms the basis for the ice-cream coupe – an idea that came from Louis Loizia, chef at Cantina del Ponte. Conran prefers silver ice-buckets, but was concerned about condensation dripping on the floor, a problem solved by fitting a bucket inside the ice-bucket to create an airspace that prevents this happening. They spent weeks getting the right cutlery and had it made to precise specifications. The same spoon is used for both soup and dessert, and the same knife and fork for every savoury course – an idea from Eric Garnier, the restaurant's General Manager. Most of the wine has to be kept chilled. This is done in a large cold room, with bottles being moved out to smaller fridges and then into ice-buckets for service. Nothing is left to chance and everything is designed.

Eric Garnier was as committed to the idea of excellence as his employers and he remains obsessed with quality. Nothing is too small to escape his eagle eye. A handsome Frenchman in his mid-thirties, who had been involved with top London restaurants for 14 years, he shared Conran's doubts about the suitability of a classic brasserie operation in an English context. 'The people who eat out in London simply will not put up with the standard of food and service that are typical in Parisian brasseries which, let's face it, are not fantastic restaurants. They have great ambience and are fine places to enjoy a drink and a snack, but it is all to do with the culture and what people expect. The French go for, say, just a plate of oysters and a glass of wine, where here people go out for a meal which includes side dishes and this complicates the whole operation. They will not tolerate a 60-minute wait in the bar for a table as they do at La Coupole. Quaglino's size must impose certain limitations, but scale does not remove the oxygen of service. Even when you are going flat

out, it is still possible to smile. I look round sometimes and I see a waiter concentrating so hard the face is frozen. Then I take that person aside after the service and remind him or her in no uncertain terms of their duty, which includes a welcome, to smile and to say goodbye. There has to be warmth in the service and eye contact. All these small things help define the customer experience.'

The choice of chef was always going to be a crucial decision, because without good food consistently delivered, all the smiles in the world will not fill a restaurant. Martin Webb had been working at Le Pont de La Tour as sous chef to David Burke and when Conran asked Burke if anybody sprang to mind as a candidate for the Quaglino's job he unhesitatingly recommended Webb. Conran remembers being immediately impressed. 'Martin had an air of calm authority and knew at once what we wanted to do. He was clearly not a prima donna, a trait unfortunately all too common among chefs these days and one that could not be tolerated here. There are 202 staff at Quag's and it has to run as a team effort. It is no place for an

insecure individual whose principal interest is self-publicity. Martin is self-effacing and I liked the fact that despite his comprehensive talents he was not at all complacent, as he has proved by the way he has striven to improve and improve the food he serves as we have gone along; and in his choice of dishes and understanding of them he is right far more often than he is wrong...'

The real countdown began six weeks before opening day, but the kitchen had still not cooked any food. Webb started taking on chefs and Conran and Kissin began going in to taste food as the kitchen got to work. 'We would come down and try as many as 20 dishes at a time. At the same time waiters were being trained. We would sit at different tables and do the whole thing as if we were customers, with the order being processed and the food cooked to order. It was incredibly exciting, for suddenly all this brilliant food was coming out, dish after dish. We'd taste and say, that's spot on or that isn't quite right.' Some things they wanted initially, like choucroute, never quite worked

out, but both felt that what was being achieved far exceeded their highest expectations.

The instant success and the quality of the food brought with it some unexpected problems, as Eric Garnier explains. 'Unlike the brasserie, where they are in and out, people like to sit for too long. In an ideal world we would be turning the tables three times during a night, but are lucky if we manage twice because people want to come and have a relaxed time, which is understandable. And everybody wants to eat at 8.30pm. We know how long the average meal takes, but can still get it wrong from time to time and you have to build in some leeway. Before we got our computer reservations system right we were getting up to 150 no-shows a night. The earliest bookings are the most difficult. If people come before 7.00pm then we have to make it clear to them that we need the table back in 1 hour 45 minutes. But the pace has to be there, it has to be fast and furious, though the customer's perception has forced us to change in certain ways. The food just goes on improving and there is a

The eight columns which bestride the restaurant are the only physical reminders of the original Quaglino's. Individually painted by eight different artists, however, they make a statement today which pays homage to La Coupole in Paris, the brasserie which first thought of decorating in such an original way. Each has been done in a style uniquely that of the artist responsible. The artists are Peter Marsh (far left), Philip Hughes (above, left), Jane Harris (above, right), Estelle Thompson, Catherine Keraly, Patrick Kinmouth, Michael Daykin, and Javaid Alvi.

Coloured tassels hang from the backs of the restaurant chairs. During evening service, staff use them as a means of identifying which tables have been fully re-laid, placing the tassel on the chair seat until each setting is complete.

QUAGLINO'S
REBORN

tremendous emphasis on the quality of service. We have cut down on the number of big tables, which are just too difficult to manage. Tables over eight can't really have a conversation in the evening anyway because of the hubbub. And if you·get a no-show on a table of 12 you cannot fill that table though you do not have a problem with a four or six.'

Time shifted at an alarming speed and the issue of which restaurant opened first still had to be resolved. They decided it was more practical to open Le Pont de la Tour first, which happened on 4 October 1991. Conran wanted to open his new Paris shop next, so Quaglino's finally opened on 14 February 1993. His assumptions about the recession being over by then were wrong as a generality, but the timing was interest-ing. Indeed, various journalists flagged the opening of Quaglino's as a gesture of confidence that the corner had been turned. 'People wrote that it was a glittering commitment to a better tomorrow and this really grabbed the public's imagination during some very grim times. We opened in an explosion of confidence and while I would not say we triggered economic recovery single-handedly we certainly played an important sym-bolic role for a lot of people. Our official opening stretched across that Valentine's weekend in 1993, after two days of previews with invited guests. Then we had some days where the restaurant was open to the public, but where the food was half price. People booking on those days were warned that there would be problems and that they were helping get things right and train the staff.' Joel Kissin had no idea whether or not he would need to advertise. In the event the press did everything for them. 'We invited 15 people to a press conference of whom nine showed up. It was the only piece of PR we did, apart from a little full-colour booklet that was Terence's idea. We printed 75,000 of them, which was paid for by Amex. We also did some limited advertising on Jazz FM. What really kick-started things was a full-page piece in *The Times* by Robin Young six weeks before we opened, and then the press went into a frenzy. We have not stopped or looked back since.'

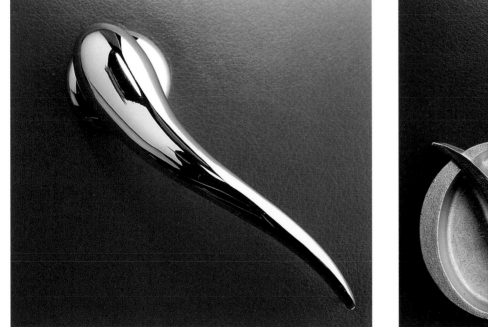

The wing nuts used to support mirrors have a sculptural quality (above, top). Polished-steel handles by Philippe Starck are used on the lavatory doors (above, left). Restaurant branding is followed through even to the ashtrays and the salt-and-pepper containers designed by Terence and Sebastian Conran (above, right).

A DAY IN THE LIFE OF...

02:30 As the door closes behind the last customers Quaglino's day is about to begin. Doormen are not as common at restaurants as they once were in smart London.

Quaglino's doormen are a reminder that a courteous greeting and help to find a cab on departure play an important part in the dining experience.

A DAY IN
THE LIFE OF ...

05:00 The service – the time when customers are actually being served food and drink – is obviously when every restaurant is working at peak activity, but at Quaglino's the behind-the-scenes activity goes on 24 hours a day with the support service staff beginning their vital duties even as the door is closed after the last customer. In a real sense this is when the restaurant's day begins, with every inch of every surface being cleaned. First deliveries start around 6.00am, and by the time the chefs begin to arrive at 7.00am to start cooking, for some night staff the day is coming to an end (above, left, and far left).

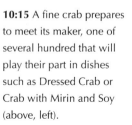

07:30 Deliveries must be checked against orders and this responsibility falls to the sous chef. Quag's has a special 'goods inwards' team who check every item for weight and quality. If something isn't right then it goes back and the supplier will suffer the chef's displeasure (left, above).

10:00 The rotisserie and charcoal grill area is a hot and demanding spot. A chef bastes lamb on the grill, causing flames to shoot up (left, below).

10:15 A fine crab prepares to meet its maker, one of several hundred that will play their part in dishes such as Dressed Crab or Crab with Mirin and Soy (above, left).

11:00 Boned rabbit legs wrapped in prosciutto are a Quag's signature dish (left).

12:00 Runners queue up to collect plated food from the pass. It is their job to take the food from the kitchen to the correct waiter stations as quickly as possible (above, right).

13:00 Total concentration under pressure distinguishes the best chefs. As the service peaks, everybody is pushed to the limit. Each knows their responsibilities and works at breathtaking speed (left).

13:30 The cold-larder team assemble salads with frantic haste, but to precise specifications. Each salad has its different ingredients and dressing. On this occasion the giant squeezy bottle contains Quag's house dressing (above).

14:00 Leaning over the balcony one has a bird's-eye view of the tables beneath. These two are tucking into a splendid *plateau de fruits de mer* (above).

14:30 One of the hardest jobs in any kitchen is washing up. Even at Quaglino's, keeping a sense of humour is not easy (right).

16:30 In the professional kitchen, moments of relaxation are brief. A cigarette on the fire escape or snatching a few minutes sleep is as much as you can hope for (above and left).

19:00 The pass is where the food comes together from all over the kitchen. It is here that it is plated, garnished and collated as a single course-order for a specific table (above).

21:00 The bar is a great place to hang out. It is busiest at night, though the numbers are carefully controlled for comfort and safety (above).

21:30 A *plateau de fruits de mer* is carried at shoulder height to a waiting table. The waiter collects and manages his orders from his waiter station which also holds fresh linen and cutlery (left).

23:00 Girls just want to have fun and Quag's is the perfect spot (overleaf).

23:30 Ask the cigarette girl if her role is submissive or sexist and you may get a short answer. Terence Conran is an enthusiastic cigar smoker and believes that tobacco in a restaurant is not a problem provided that the air conditioning works properly as it does at Quag's (far left).

24:00 When Quag's opened in 1929, cocktails were in their heyday. People started to enjoy them again 20 years ago and they have gradually increased in popularity ever since. Now the barmen will fix whatever takes your fancy, including, of course, a Quaglino's champagne cup, the cocktail invented by John Quaglino for the 1929 opening. The dispense bar is also where finger bowls are filled to go out with the *plateaux de fruits de mer* (centre, above and below).

01:00 A final coffee at the bar. Cappuccino is a must these days and the froth stands high enough to spoon (right).

RECIPES

Martin Webb was born in Wigan, Lancashire, the son of a stonemason, and was first apprenticed locally in the kitchen of The Brocket Arms in June 1976 at the age of 16. Within a year he found himself in charge of a hotel kitchen in Gloucestershire and after another year joined the brigade at The Belfry Club in Halkin Street. This was followed by a stint as a pastry-chef in the Alpine resort of Tignes, then increasingly senior assignments in English kitchens. After a year cooking seafood in Jersey he went to Perth, Western Australia for six months, and returned to England again only to emigrate to Perth in 1982. In the next nine years he ran a number of restaurants, gaining wide recognition for his cooking and winning The Golden Plate, Western Australia's most prestigious food award, on three separate occasions and for three different restaurants. In 1986 he opened his own Café Polperro in Fremantle, before taking over The Ord Street Café in Perth. He returned to London in 1991, joining the team at Le Pont de la Tour as junior sous chef, soon being promoted to sous chef. Before opening Quaglino's he was involved with every aspect of the kitchen's design.

Although 10 years ago I thought myself to be very open minded in my approach to cooking, I suspect I was quite inflexible; but then when you look back, you constantly revise the past in terms of where you are today. In Australia I ran small restaurants where I enjoyed a one-to-one relationship with customers which was very rewarding. Obviously doing 1,000 covers a day that just isn't possible at Quaglino's. Yet being able to deliver quality on such a scale is based largely on my experience in small restaurants. Running my own place taught me about the business side — the importance of attention to detail and all the tough accountancy disciplines. Most importantly, though, it taught me about being a restaurateur and focusing on my customers, listening to what they wanted. You cannot produce good food for long unless you do so in a business-like way. And you must never lose sight of why you are doing it.

In Perth, what I cooked was what was available in the market, but increasingly what I wanted to eat. As a chef there, you had to work harder at being more imaginative. You also had to have the command of basic skills in butchery, fish and pastry. We are fortunate in London, I can specify precise weights and cuts, buy duck and rabbit legs for confit, reject anything that does not exactly meet my criteria. And, as all my suppliers will tell you, I am very demanding.

Cooking in Western Australia is very Asian-influenced, with great fresh produce coming in all the time. The fruit there is second to none and the fish marvellous. Small Thai, Vietnamese, Malay and Indonesian restaurants are everywhere, producing authentic food that is excellent value. It is all so fresh and honest and completely informal, a world away from the restaurants of my apprentice days where you couldn't make a legitimate complaint unless you were wearing a suit and tie. The opportunity to travel throughout Asia brought with it the chance to compare the real thing with what I had been eating in Perth. It inspired me, not to copy dishes but to find new directions, putting what I learned into a different idiom. First you have to understand the source and respect its authenticity. It's like what's happening with Indian restaurants in Britain, dressing them up to be something they were never intended to be. There is often a confusion between appearance on one level and delivery on another. Tablecloths and a maître d'hôtel in a dinner jacket don't upgrade the food. A restaurant can be very serious about its food yet informal, which is something different from being casual.

Chefs aren't artists, and when they believe they are watch out, because the food is going to be pretentious. I may like painting and drawing, but that does not make me an artist in the kitchen. The skills involved are closer to an artisan than an artist. The kind of chef who spends hours carving a stag's head out of butter demonstrates skill, but inappropriately. Go and carve a tombstone, I'd say. If you want to be a chef then taste must come first. Taste and balance are the real issues.

Before we opened, my first reaction on being asked to produce food based on classic French brasserie dishes was that this was a step backwards to cover old ground, but I was wrong. There were new challenges and opportunities for redefinition. Look at the boudins blancs we make ourselves and the terrines. Then there are points of departure, like the Crab with Mirin and Soy, which takes the freshest dressed shellfish and presents it with subtle references to my own Southeast Asian influences. As time has gone by, I have proved that different styles of dishes can work happily in the Quaglino's environment. Of course, it can never be and should never be a Pacific Rim restaurant, but it is a place where we can surprise people by being ambitious and delivering the goods. But the execution has to be spot on. The idea alone is not enough. If it's not right then people will say, 'trying too hard, stick to what you can do'.

The food on the customer's plate will always be the most important thing, but what the customer does not see is also important. The kitchen is spotlessly clean at all times and my chefs are too. If people are dirty or slovenly then that is going to have a knock-on effect. I have a team, and the people in it are proud of themselves and have respect for one another. That respect is based on discipline. I hate kitchens where people are messing about. Sloppy behaviour is dangerous, and without complete concentration mistakes will happen and you will lose consistent delivery. I don't want one table to be perfect and another fall short of the mark.

I disapprove of ego in the kitchen. Having the confidence that comes from knowing you are good is one thing, getting hung up on the media is another. It's nice to have compliments, but I know that all my life I would rather be criticized by an expert than praised by a fool. That being said, you have to have the courage of your own convictions or some of the criticism can lay you low. After 20 years working at something you should be professional at what you do. You should in the end be your own worst critic. I understand what I am about and my goal is simple – to enjoy cooking food well. That comes not only from putting in the time but also from thinking about what you have done and why. Understanding simplicity as something profound means you produce dishes for the right reasons, food which stems from confidence. I now know that you can't do better than a perfectly roasted squab with a simple jus. If you dress it up too much then you miss the point of its beauty and obscure the perfection of the raw material. That is the sensitivity that comes with maturity and implies a clarity of vision that can only be gained when arrogance has been overcome.

If you cook good food every day of your life and give people pleasure, then you are doing well. Chefs who have innate talent and learn sensitivity will, in time, develop a discernible personal style. When you are younger you get lost in the technicalities, want to show off your skills, and lose sight of the person eating the dish and what they want from it. Skill is not something to be judged in isolation. The intensity of a reduction can become an end in itself, which misses the point by a mile when its richness overpowers the rest of a dish. Everything on the plate must be in harmony. The different elements are there because they work together well and for no other reason.

I believe that chefs should travel and experience the world beyond the kitchen, and should eat out as often and as widely as possible. Since Norman times the only successful invasions of this country have been culinary, and today we can show the world how well we have learned from those ethnic examples.

I am proud of Quaglino's and to be part of the renaissance taking place in British cooking.

STARTERS

OYSTERS

Quaglino's serves an average of 5,000 raw oysters every week, both native flat oysters – the finest in the world, but very expensive and difficult to get hold of to eat at home – and Pacific rock oysters. Pacific rock oysters are more readily available and about half the price, though purists would say with good reason. Buy them from your fishmonger or by mail order. You will be sold them surrounded with seaweed and they will stay happily alive in the fridge for several days if kept damp. Don't be scared of opening them yourself, though you will find it easier to do the job without damaging yourself or the bivalves if you use an oyster knife.

To open, put the oyster on a flat surface with the flatter half of the shell upwards and hinged end towards you. Hold the other end firmly in a cloth with one hand and with the other, ease the tip of a knife into the small opening in the hinge. Wiggle the tip until it gives. Once inserted, twist the handle and lever the shell open. Restaurants in this country tend to sever the muscle which attaches the oyster to the shell, flipping it over before serving. This is an unnecessary refinement. A small fork is the best thing to eat them with.

'Our oysters, both natives and Pacifics, come from Ireland. We serve them with shallot vinegar, lemon juice and Tabasco, all for people to help themselves. You can buy shallot vinegars or make a more acceptable version yourself as follows:

Peel 6 shallots, slice them thinly and then dice them. Put into a bowl and add 4 tablespoons of red wine vinegar, 2 teaspoons of sugar and 1/4 teaspoon of salt. Stir and leave to marinate at room temperature for 1 hour.

To serve, arrange the opened oysters on crushed ice or seaweed. Put a half lemon for each person and small individual ramekins of shallot relish next to each place.' MW

DRESSED CRAB WITH MIRIN & SOY

This is one of the restaurant's most popular and enduring first courses and a key to its success is the absolute freshness of the crabs. Bought-in dressed crab will never taste as good. The richness that is always part of even the simplest crab dish is balanced by the unusual salad, which is made from wakame – a Japanese seaweed. Dashi is stock made from bonito flakes (dried fish) and konbu seaweed can be bought in sachets. Mirin is sweet rice wine. All of these are obtainable from Japanese markets and most of them from Chinese markets.

INGREDIENTS FOR 4
2 crabs, each weighing about 900g / 2lb,
   cooked and prepared as described on page 93
1/2 cucumber
115g / 4oz pack of wakame
2 limes

for the crab dressing:
3 1/2 tbsp rice wine vinegar
3 1/2 tbsp dashi
120ml / 4fl oz / 1/2 cup mirin
2 tbsp Kikkoman soy sauce

for the salad dressing:
120ml / 4fl oz rice wine vinegar
5 tbsp Kikkoman soy sauce
15g / 1/2oz / 1 tbsp sugar

Prepare the crabs, reserving all the white flaky crab meat and 4 tablespoons of brown meat. Use the remaining crab in another dish and use the shells for fish stock or crustacea oil (page 139).

Peel the cucumber, cut it in half lengthwise and scrape out the seeds with a teaspoon. Slice it as thinly as possible (use a mandoline grater if you have one). Put the slices into a bowl, salt lightly and leave for 2 hours. Rinse in a sieve under cold running water and reserve.

Make the crab dressing: in a small pan, bring all the ingredients to the boil. Remove from the heat and allow to cool. Make the salad dressing in the same way.

Put the wakame to soak for 10 minutes in tepid water. Wash in cold water, pick the leaves off the stem and put to dry on a clean cloth. Then transfer to a bowl with the cucumber. Toss gently with your fingers to mix.

On each of 4 large serving plates, put a pile of white crab meat, a spoonful of brown meat and a mound of wakame salad. Put a tablespoon of the crab dressing on the white meat, and a tablespoon of the salad dressing on the wakame and cucumber. Put a half lime on each plate and serve at once.

SPICY THAI MACKEREL SALAD

Thai salads are distinguished in their homeland by the abundance of edible leaves and flowers that grow in that part of the world and nowhere else. An understanding of the nature of what you are making is more important than a slavish search for authentic ingredients, though in some cases substitution is not acceptable. For example, Thai or Vietnamese mint has a unique flavour and, in this recipe, if you cannot find any in an Oriental market, leave it out. The basil is Thai holy basil, also called purple basil.

'The recipe specifies banana shallots, but any shallots will do. Other shallots are smaller, however, so double the number. The amount of chilli you use is up to your and your guests' taste buds. They vary so much in their heat it is always advisable to taste before following the number specified in any recipe. The amount given is therefore only a rough guide.' MW

INGREDIENTS FOR 4

2 mackerel, each weighing about 350g / 12oz, gutted and with heads removed
4 banana shallots

5 cm / 2 in piece of root ginger
4 fresh red chillies
4 fresh green chillies
1 green sour mango
115g / 4oz fresh coriander, including roots
6 stalks of lemon grass
2 red onions
12 Vietnamese mint leaves (optional)
12 large basil leaves
55g / 2oz / ¼ cup salted peanuts

for the dressing:
2 tbsp nam pla Thai fish sauce
4 tbsp freshly squeezed lime juice
5 tbsp sunflower oil

Poach the fish at a bare simmer in salted water for 5 minutes. Leave it to cool in the liquid.

As you prepare the salad ingredients, put them in a large bowl. Peel and chop the shallots finely. Peel the ginger and cut it in half. Cut one half into julienne strips, reserving the other half, and add the julienne to the bowl. Cut the chillies in half lengthwise and deseed. Cut these chilli halves in two lengthwise, then cut these into the finest cross-cut strips. Remove the flesh from the mango and cut it into julienne strips. Wash the coriander, making sure all dirt is scrubbed from the roots. Chop the roots finely and the leaves coarsely. Top and tail the lemon grass, then cut the stalks across into the thinnest strips, before chopping finely. Peel the onions and cut them in half lengthwise, then slice them thinly lengthwise. Add the Vietnamese mint leaves if you've managed to find them. Tear the basil into strips.

Remove the mackerel from the poaching liquid and dry on paper towels. Pull the flesh away from the skin in large chunks. Remove any small bones.

Make the dressing: grate the reserved ginger over a piece of butter muslin (cheesecloth) then squeeze it, to extract the juice, into a bowl. To the bowl add the fish sauce, lime juice and oil. Stir to mix and pour over the salad, then toss gently to dress.

Transfer the salad to a large flat serving plate and pile the fish on top. Finally, scatter over the salted peanuts and serve at room temperature.

MARINATED CHICKEN SALAD

Normally a marinade is used as a preliminary before meat is cooked, but in this dish it is applied to the cooked flesh and is then served with it as a cold sauce or dressing. There is a general tendency to roast chicken for serving it cold, but this aromatic salad with its sweet-and-sour dressing benefits from the bird being poached. This has the added advantage of producing a light stock for use in another dish. The marinade includes cloves, pine nuts and sultanas – an almost medieval combination of flavours. After cooking, the chicken is cut up and marinated for several hours to allow the complex flavours to develop fully. Ideally, prepare the dish a day in advance and marinate overnight in the fridge. It should be removed 4 hours before serving and served at room temperature.

INGREDIENTS FOR 4
1 carrot
1 onion
1 leek
1 celery stalk
**1 dressed free-range chicken, weighing about
    1.1 – 1.35kg / 2¹/₂ – 3lb**
2 bay leaves
handful of parsley stalks
10 black peppercorns
¹/₂ tbsp salt
good crusty rustic bread, to serve

for the marinade:
3 tbsp pine nuts
3 whole cloves
2 bay leaves
3 tbsp sultanas

¹/₂ tsp hot chilli flakes
175ml / 6fl oz / ³/₄ cup extra-virgin olive oil
2 tbsp red wine vinegar
juice of 1 lemon
1 tbsp sugar
salt and pepper

The day before: peel, wash, trim and coarsely chop the carrot, onion, leek and celery. Put the chicken into a saucepan in which it just fits, cover with cold water and bring to the boil. Immediately lower the heat and skim off the scum that has risen to the surface. Then add the chopped vegetables, the bay leaves, parsley stalks, peppercorns and salt. Poach at a bare simmer for 40–45 minutes, depending on the size of the chicken. Remove from the hob (stove top) and leave to cool in the liquid.

Take the bird from the pot and remove and discard all the skin and fat. Pull the flesh off the bones, tear it into strips and put in a serving bowl. Put the bones back in the stock and return to a boil. Lower the heat, skim, then poach gently for 1– 2 hours to finish the stock. Pass this through a fine sieve, let cool then refrigerate for another use.

In a dry heavy omelette pan or skillet, toast the pine nuts for 2 minutes over a low heat, stirring constantly as they burn easily and if they do you will have to throw them away and start again. Scatter them over the chicken with the cloves, the bay leaves and the sultanas. Mix the other marinade ingredients together, add salt and pepper to taste and pour over, pushing down the chicken if necessary to ensure all the pieces are completely covered. Marinate overnight in the fridge, removing 4 hours before you want to eat.

Serve with a nice crusty rustic bread. It needs nothing more.

SPINACH & PARMESAN TART

Cheese and spinach are among cooking's most serendipitous combinations and crop up in the classic French kitchen as Florentine, thereby begging the question of whether or not it was an Italian cook who first thought of putting them together in the first place.

Italy's most extraordinary cheese must be Parmesan, now available by the piece in supermarkets, but for many years only sold as a powdered and unpleasant-smelling substance purchased in small drums to be shaken sparingly over spaghetti Bolognese. Cut with a special sharp trowel from the huge rounds in which it is produced, sweet Reggiano Parmigiano is a delightful pale-yellow colour flecked with white and is the finest of the so-called grana cheeses to carry the Parmigiano name.

'We use Reggiano Parmigiano extensively. Here it is combined with just-blanched leaf spinach and bound with an egg, cream and Mascarpone liaison cooked in a crisp pastry crust until just set. You can make it well in advance and then warm it through just before serving. Eat it as a first course on its own or in a slightly larger portion with a green salad for a perfect light lunch.' MW

INGREDIENTS FOR 6

125g / 4¹/₂oz Reggiano Parmesan (in a piece)
450g / 1lb large-leaf spinach
45g / 1¹/₂oz / 3 tbsp butter
2 eggs, plus 3 extra yolks
150ml / ¹/₄pt / ²/₃ cup double (heavy) cream
125g / 4¹/₂oz Mascarpone cheese
extra-virgin olive oil, to serve (optional)
black pepper

for the pastry:
225g / 8oz / 2 cups plain (all-purpose) flour
pinch of salt
125g / 4¹/₂oz / 9 tbsp unsalted butter, chilled
2 egg yolks

Spinach & Parmesan tart

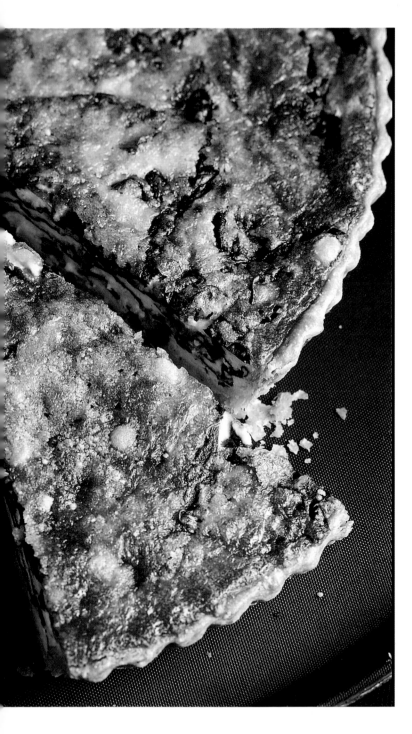

First make the pastry: sift the flour into a mixing bowl and add the pinch of salt. Take the butter from the fridge only at the last minute and cut into cubes. Add to the bowl and rub all together until you have a uniform grainy amalgamation. Whisk the egg yolks with 3$^{1}/_{2}$ tablespoons of cold water and add half of this to the bowl. Work together quickly and add the remaining liquid until it binds to form a dough. Be careful not to overwork or you will get a heavy result. Alternatively, you can make this pastry by putting the flour, salt and butter into a food processor, working until it crumbs then adding the liquid through the feeder tube until the dough balls. Cling-wrap and allow to rest in the fridge for 1 hour.

Preheat the oven to 200°C / 400°F / gas 6.

Roll the pastry out thinly and use to line a loose-bottomed 25cm / 10in tart tin. Line the pastry case with foil, fill with beans and bake blind for 10 minutes. Remove the foil and beans and return to the oven for a further 5–7 minutes until the base is uniformly cooked through. Remove when done. Lower the oven temperature to 140°C / 275°F / gas 1.

Grate the Parmesan (not too finely). Remove any large stalks from the spinach, discarding any blemished leaves. Melt the butter in a large pan and toss the leaves in it to wilt. Transfer to a colander to drain.

Beat the eggs, extra yolks, cream and Mascarpone together to a smooth custard. Spoon enough of this into the tart case to form a thin even film. Sprinkle with grated Parmesan, cover with a layer of spinach, and season with pepper, then repeat these layers until the tart is full to the brim, finishing with a gloss of custard.

Bake on a baking sheet in the oven for 20–25 minutes, or until set. Remove and leave to cool until warm, before taking off the outer ring by standing the tart on a cake tin.

Either serve immediately on warm plates with a little extra-virgin olive oil dribbled over and some more shaved Parmesan scattered on top or leave until needed, warming the tart through gently at 140°C / 275°F / gas 1.

PIGEON/SQUAB SALAD WITH PANCETTA & FLAGEOLETS

Wood pigeons (squab) have an excellent flavour and, in any case, are cheap enough to allow you to use only the breast meat in a dish. The carcasses can then be used to make very good stock.

Flageolets are the dried pale-green haricot beans and pancetta is the superior Italian bacon that is now becoming more widely available. Buy it in a piece.

INGREDIENTS FOR 4
170g / 6oz / ³/4 cup flageolets
1 bay leaf
140g / 5oz pancetta
170g / 6oz French beans
4 wood pigeons (squab)
1 head of chicory (endive)
salt and pepper

for the dressing:
150ml / ¹/4pt / ²/3 cup extra-virgin olive oil
2 tbsp shallot vinegar

The day before: put the flageolet beans to soak in plenty of cold water.

The next day: bring the beans to the boil, drain through a colander, rinse in cold water and return to the pan. Cover with cold water by about 2.5cm / 1in. Add the bay leaf, bring to the boil and immediately lower the heat to a simmer. Cook for 60–90 minutes until tender, seasoning with salt and pepper only towards the end of the cooking time. Remove from the heat and leave to cool in the liquid.

Preheat the oven to its highest setting.

Cut the pancetta into lardons and dry-fry them gently in a non-stick pan until crisp. Remove from the pan and drain on paper towels.

Top and tail the French beans and blanch for 3–4 minutes in rapidly boiling water. Refresh in cold water and reserve.

In a roasting pan over medium heat, seal the pigeons in the bacon fat, turning to get a good colour. Transfer to the oven, breast sides up and give them 8 minutes. They should be very pink. Remove and reserve. Drain off any cooking juices and reserve.

Make the dressing by whisking the oil and vinegar with the roasting pan juices until emulsified. Season, reserve and cool, but do not refrigerate.

Toss the French beans with the flageolets, the pancetta and the dressing. Taste and adjust seasoning.

Cut the breasts from the pigeons and then cut each across into two. Remove the legs and cut off the meat. Add to the beans and toss.

Put 3–4 chicory leaves on each plate with the beans, pigeon and pancetta mounded on top. Finish with a few turns of black pepper.

TOMATO & MOZZARELLA WITH AUBERGINE/EGGPLANT PESTO

Unusually, the aubergine (eggplant) in this dish is cut into very small dice and fried until it firms up, losing all moisture and becoming like a crisp vegetable mince.

The aubergine pesto will keep in a screw-top jar in the fridge for ages if you film the surface with a little more of the olive oil. It is a delicious addition to many dishes, not to mention a classic pasta sauce in its own right.

'The fresher the Mozzarella the better, and it really should be the best buffalo-milk cheese you can buy. Good Italian delicatessens are the best source.' MW

INGREDIENTS FOR 4
6 ripe plum tomatoes
1 large aubergine (eggplant)
100ml / 3¹/2fl oz / ¹/2 cup extra-virgin olive oil
3 buffalo Mozzarella cheeses
salt and pepper

for the pesto:

75g / 2¹/₂oz / 5 cups basil leaves
45g / 1¹/₂oz / 3 cups flat-leaf parsley leaves
55g / 2oz / ¹/₄ cup pine nuts
4 garlic cloves
75g / 2¹/₂oz / ³/₄ cup Parmesan cheese, grated
300ml / ¹/₂pt / 1¹/₄ cups extra-virgin olive oil
ciabatta, sourdough bread or baguette, to serve

First make the pesto: put all the ingredients except the Parmesan and oil in a food processor and blitz to an even-textured crumb. Add the cheese, followed by the oil in a thin stream through the feeder tube. Taste and season with salt and pepper.

Blanch the tomatoes briefly in boiling water, refresh in cold water and peel. Peel and chop the aubergine as finely as you can.

Heat 4 tablespoons of the oil in a heavy frying pan. When hot, add the aubergine and stir-fry until it starts to crisp and brown lightly. Place in a sieve to drain. Then, while still hot, transfer to a bowl and stir in 6 table-spoons of the pesto together with the remaining olive oil. Grind in some black pepper.

Cut the tomatoes and Mozzarella across into slices and arrange, overlapping them in concentric circles on 4 plates.

Spoon over the aubergine pesto and finish with more black pepper. Serve with ciabatta or baguette.

SMOKED BACON & TRUFFLE PÂTÉ

While Quaglino's chefs use pancetta for this dish you can use smoked streaky bacon. Its quality will deter-mine how exceptional the end-product will be, and the fattier the bacon used in this dish the better. Supermarkets are making some effort in response to a growing public distaste for the bath-brined bacon and chemical flavourings of mass-production, but they still have a long way to go. When seasoning the pâté, remember that the bacon may be very salty.

'The truffles included in this recipe are tinned truffle trimmings. If you happened to have the odd fresh black truffle handy then by all means substitute. For the glaze we use veal stock, port and Madeira, enriched and jellied with pigs' trot-ters. This version uses chicken stock.' MW

INGREDIENTS FOR 8

450g / 1lb chicken livers
550g / 1¹/₄lb smoked (thick-sliced) bacon
115g / 4oz pork fillet
150ml / ¹/₄pt / ²/₃ cup Cognac
3 tsp quatre-épices (see page 74)
3 tsp salt
3 tsp ground black pepper
10 egg yolks
750ml / 1¹/₄pt / 3 cups double (heavy) cream
55g / 2oz / ¹/₄ cup tinned black truffle pieces
1 tbsp cracked black peppercorns
butter, for greasing

for the glaze:

1 pig's trotter (foot), split and cut into pieces
1.1 litre / 2pt / 5 cups chicken stock (see page 138)
150ml / ¹/₄pt / ²/₃ cup port
1 tbsp chopped fresh thyme
8 black peppercorns
1 bay leaf

At least 2 days before serving: clean the chicken livers, cutting off and discarding any tubes or green bits. Cut the bacon into lardon strips, then cut these across into small rectangles and put in a food processor. Dice the pork and add it to the bacon. Work to a purée. Add the chicken livers, Cognac, spices and seasoning and work again to incorporate to a smooth paste. Scrape into a bowl, cover and refrigerate for 30 minutes. If you have the kind of processor that allows you to remove and refit a filled bowl, then simply put this in the fridge.

Preheat the oven to 180°C / 350°F / gas 4.

Whisk the egg yolks in a large bowl then add the cream, whisking to amalgamate to a smooth custard. Switch on the processor at half speed and add the custard to the meat purée through the feeder tube. As soon as you have a uniform mix, switch off and pour and scrape into a bowl. Fold in the truffle trimmings.

Butter a rectangular terrine, line the bottom with a piece of greaseproof paper and fill the dish with the mixture to within 2cm / 3/4in of the top. Put on the lid and bake in a bain-marie for 50–60 minutes, when it will be firm but pliant to the touch. Remove, let cool and then refrigerate for 24 hours.

The next day: make the glaze. Put the trotter into a pan, cover with cold water and bring to the boil. A lot of scum will be produced. Throw this away with the water and rinse the trotter.

Return to the pan with all the other meat glaze ingredients. Bring to the boil, skim, lower the heat and simmer for 2 hours, topping up with water if necessary. Strain the liquid through a fine sieve into a clean pan and return to a boil and reduce until it has a good thick coating consistency.

Leave to cool.

Sprinkle the cracked pepper on top of the pâté, then pour over the cooled glaze and return to the fridge overnight or for up to 7 days. Repeat the glazing process if necessary.

The day of serving: turn out the pâté by dipping the terrine in very hot water and sliding a knife around the edge. Serve in slices with rustic bread or toast.

FOIE GRAS TERRINE

The critical thing when cooking foie gras is the temperature. Allow it to rise above 70°C / 158°F and the liver will literally melt.

Unusually, Quaglino's cooks the foie gras in a tray on the hob (stove top) and not in a bain-marie in the oven. You must use a thermometer to check the temperature of the goose fat in which the liver is poached.

Everybody knows how expensive it is, but how to tell whether you are paying for prime foie gras? If it breaks easily, it has an unusually high fat content that will exude in large quantities during cooking. On the other hand, a liver which is very elastic will be rather fibrous and have a poor flavour. With a perfect liver, the flesh stretches gently before falling apart.

'This technique for cooking foie gras is the best I have ever come across and delivers a beautiful pink-and-yellow-tinged terrine with a perfect buttery consistency. We wear surgical gloves when handling the livers because the temperatures used in cooking them are too low to kill bacteria.' MW

INGREDIENTS FOR 12

2 raw fresh foie gras duck livers, weighing about 675g / 1 1/2lb each
450g / 1lb goose fat
butter, for greasing
toasted brioche, to serve

for the marinade:
4 tbsp port
4 tbsp Armagnac or brandy
1/2 tsp grated nutmeg
15g / 1/2oz / 1 tbsp Maldon sea salt
1 tsp milled black pepper

Day 1: because of their high fat content the livers will have stiffened in the fridge, so remove them and allow them to soften at room temperature until you have a pliant consistency. This is a critical moment because, if left too long, they will literally begin to melt and will not break cleanly into pieces. If this starts to happen, return them to the fridge briefly.

Carefully separate the lobes with your hands to give you 4 pieces of liver – 2 large and 2 small. With a blunt round-ended knife, cut each piece open, making one incision from top to bottom and then a second incision from left to right to make a cross. Using the same knife, gently pull back each quarter until you reach the vein. Scrape carefully along the length of the vein and lift away in one piece. Discard the waste and repeat with the other lobes.

Scrape away any green contamination from the gall bladder. Return to the fridge for 15 minutes to firm again. This makes the next stage easier.

Break the liver into pieces about 7.5 x 2.5 cm / 3 x 1 in. Place the pieces in a bowl, and then spoon over the port and Armagnac or brandy, and sprinkle with the nutmeg, salt, and pepper.

Cling-wrap and refrigerate overnight.

Day 2: butter a 25 x 10cm / 10 x 4in rectangular terrine and line it with cling-film.

Remove the duck livers from the fridge an hour before you want to cook them in order to bring them up to room temperature.

Place the goose fat in a pan and melt it very gently over a low heat until it reaches a temperature of 50°C / 122°F.

Add the foie gras a few pieces at a time. Move them around gently to ensure even cooking. If you put them all in at once it will lower the temperature too much. You can tell when they are done by the change in colour and texture, which takes 1–2 minutes. Remove the pieces with your fingers and reserve.

When all are done and while still warm, fill the terrine, laying the largest pieces in the bottom.

Cut a piece of cardboard to the exact size of the top of the surface and cover it in foil. Place this on top and weight it down with a 450g / 1lb weight (do not exceed this weight).

Refrigerate overnight.

Day 3: remove the terrine from the fridge. Melt some of the poaching fat and pour a 2mm / $^1\!/_{12}$in layer on the top of the terrine. Return to the fridge for at least a further 24 hours before serving. Uncut it will keep for up to 2 weeks.

The day of serving: to turn out, dip the terrine for 3–4 seconds in a bowl of hot water. Turn upside down and tug on the cling-film to remove, then peel away the film.

Dip a sharp knife in boiling water to warm the blade and use to cut the terrine across into 1cm / $^1\!/_2$in thick slices. Serve with toasted brioche.

TERRINE DE CAMPAGNE

Forcefully flavoured liver-based pâtés have rather gone out of fashion on restaurant menus, but this very French country-style terrine is an enduring Quaglino's favourite. It is distinguished by its defining ingredients, which include wood pigeon (squab), rabbit and foie gras. Slightly less than half the meats are retained as dice, which are set into a minced (ground) farce or forcemeat. This gives both contrasting textures and visual appeal.

Buy foie gras trimmings if you can; and wood pigeon (squab), which is very cheap. Only the breasts are used, but a good stock can be made with the carcasses. The restaurant uses a rabbit jus, but you can substitute a strong chicken stock and, while it will never be as nice as the flesh from a whole rabbit, you may find it convenient to substitute frozen cubed rabbit in this recipe.

It is important to weigh the ingredients carefully to

Terrine de campagne

make sure that you have the right proportion of cubed meats to minced (ground) farce.

When weighting terrines, never put too heavy a weight on top or you will squeeze all the moisture and fat out, leaving you with a dry result. A good thing to do is to have a piece of wood which will just fit the top surface, then stand a 450g / 1lb can on top. Alternatively, cut a piece of cardboard and cover it in foil, then weight it.

Before cutting the terrine into slices, leave the pâté to mature in the fridge for between 3 and 7 days for maximum benefit.

'Quatre-épices is the mixture of white pepper, nutmeg, cloves and cinnamon or ginger which is widely used in classic French charcuterie. The precise ratios depend on personal preference, but pepper should always predominate. Make it yourself by mixing 100g / 3¹/₂oz / ³/₄ cup white peppercorns, 30g / 1oz / ¹/₂ cup nutmeg, 30g / 1oz / ¹/₂ cup ground ginger and 8g /¹/₄oz / 4 tsp cloves. Put the peppercorns, nutmeg and cloves into a coffee grinder and pulverize to a fine powder. Put with the ginger in a screw-top jar and give it a shake. It will keep forever but, like all ground spices, will deteriorate and lose pungency with time, so it is best to use it within 3 months.' MW

INGREDIENTS FOR 8–10

550g / 1¹/₄lb rabbit meat
550g / 1¹/₄lb chicken livers
170g / 6oz pork back fat
4 pigeon breasts (squab), about 55g / 2oz each
350g / 12oz foie gras
4 garlic cloves
1 tbsp flat-leaf parsley leaves
2 tbsp Armagnac or Cognac
150ml / ¹/₄pt / ²/₃ cup dry white wine
100ml / 3¹/₂fl oz / ¹/₂ rabbit cup jus or reduced chicken stock
4 tsp quatre-épices
1 tbsp sea salt
caul fat for wrapping

Day 1: Cut the meat into 1cm / ¹/₂in cubes, then weigh into 2 batches; 1 to retain as dice and the other to mince through the fine plate of a mincer (grinder) as follows: 425g / 15oz rabbit; 325g / 11oz chicken livers; 140g / 5oz back fat; 225g / 8oz foie gras.

Peel, smash and finely chop the garlic and chop the parsley. Put all the meats, diced and minced, in a large bowl. Add the garlic, parsley, Armagnac, white wine, rabbit jus and quatre-épices and mulch it all together with your hands. Press down gently, cover with cling-wrap and refrigerate overnight.

Day 2: preheat the oven to 180°C / 350°F / gas 4.

Heat a frying pan. Take 1 tablespoon of the mixture and fry it on both sides for a couple of minutes until cooked, leave it to cool, then eat it. This is the only way to judge whether you have seasoned the terrine mixture properly. Since you need more seasoning when things are eaten cold rather than hot, it is important to leave your tasting sample until it is cool. Adjust with more salt and pepper if needed.

Line a 1.7 litre / 3 pint / 7¹/₂ cup terrine or a large non-stick loaf tin with the caul, and add the mixture, folding the caul over the top. Cover, place in a bain-marie and fill one-third of the way up with hot water.

Bake for 1¹/₂ hours, then test by pushing a skewer into the centre of the terrine. Leave it there for 30 seconds, then pull it out and touch it. If it feels hot, then it is done. If not, give it another 10–15 minutes and then check again.

Remove from the oven and leave to cool, placing a 450g / 1lb weight on top. When cold enough, refrigerate for at least 3 days and for up to a week.

CHICKEN LIVER
& FOIE GRAS PARFAIT

Chicken livers need to be treated carefully if they are not to become dense and strongly flavoured when cooked. The standard chicken liver terrine is too often presented as a solid chilled block, but who likes the idea of chicken liver ice-cream? This much lighter variation on the theme incorporates some duck foie gras, which gives a luxurious dimension. The strength of taste is moderated by incorporating a high percentage of butter and the mousse is cooked at a very low temperature, until just set.

'This low temperature is essential or most of the fat exudes from the foie gras and will set in a deep slab on the top of the parfait. It goes without saying that it is very rich and only a small slice is needed. Ideally, serve it with rustic bread or toasted sourdough bread.' MW

INGREDIENTS FOR 10–12

350g / 12oz chicken livers
85g / 3oz / 1 small onion
1 small garlic clove
250g / 9oz / 2 sticks + 2 tbsp unsalted butter
100ml / 3¹/2fl oz / ¹/2 cup dry white wine
1 bay leaf
2 sprigs of thyme
115g / 4oz fresh foie gras
1 egg
¹/4 nutmeg, grated
1 tbsp Madeira
1 tbsp port
1 tbsp Cognac
8g / ¹/4oz / 1 tbsp green peppercorns
salt and pepper

Pick over the chicken livers, cutting away any green-tinged parts, all tubes and fatty membranes. Put the livers to soak in milk for 30 minutes. This removes bitter juices. (There is less need to do this if the livers are very clean to start with.) Transfer to a sieve, rinse under cold running water and put to drain.

Preheat the oven to 110°C / 225°F / gas ¹/4. Cut a piece of greaseproof paper to line the bottom of a small terrine. Alternatively, use a non-stick loaf tin. Stand this in a roasting tin and pour in water to come halfway up the sides of the terrine or loaf tin.

Peel the onion and garlic. Cut into fine dice and sweat in 30g / 1oz / 2 tbsp of the butter in a frying pan over gentle heat, until soft. Add the white wine with the bay leaf and thyme and reduce at a fast boil until you are left with only a moist residue in the pan. Remove the bay and thyme. Pass through a fine sieve into a food processor and add the chicken livers, foie gras and egg, with the grated nutmeg. Liquidize.

In a small saucepan over a moderate heat, reduce the Madeira, port and Cognac by half. Add to the liver mixture, together with the peppercorns. Season to taste. (If you want to, quickly dry-fry a spoonful and taste for seasoning.)

At the same time, melt the remaining butter over a low flame in a small pan. Increase the heat and bring to the boil. Slowly add the melted butter to the liquidized liver mixture through the feeder tube. Immediately pass through a fine sieve into the terrine or loaf tin. (If you leave it to cool you will have difficulty getting it through the sieve.)

Bake for 25 minutes or until just set. Remove, let cool and then refrigerate.

To turn out, dip the terrine for 3–4 seconds in a bowl of hot water before turning upside down. Serve the parfait with Onion confit (page 141) and crusty bread. To make serving easier, dip a sharp knife in hot water before cutting the slices.

SEARED SALMON WITH HERBED POTATO SALAD

It was the Japanese who first showed us how good salmon is eaten raw and the appropriateness of tataki – searing the outside briefly to leave the centre uncooked and moist. However you treat it, the quality of the fish is very important now that salmon farming is delivering some of the cheapest and nastiest protein on earth. That being said, the best farmed variety can be indistinguishable from wild salmon, if it is fed decently and grown in locations with a fast-running current.

'Ask your fishmonger to trim the fish for you and remove the pin bones. These are not difficult tasks, particularly if you use a strong pair of tweezers, and it does not matter whether you have your fillet cut from the head or tail end, though the tail end is easier to deal with if you have to do it yourself.

The potato salad is ideally made with new potatoes like Jersey Royals, the first of the crop taken before they have formed a proper skin. If you are making this later in the year, peel the potatoes.' MW

INGREDIENTS FOR 4
**16 new potatoes
1 small bunch of chives, cut into 2.5cm / 1in pieces
1 tsp torn sage leaves
1 tbsp torn basil leaves
1 tbsp chopped flat-leaf parsley
1 tsp oregano leaves (optional, but don't use dried)
125ml / 4fl oz / $^{1}/_{2}$ cup extra-virgin olive oil
550g / 14oz fillet of salmon
salt and pepper**

for the aïoli:
**1 large garlic clove
2 egg yolks
300ml / $^{1}/_{2}$pt / 1$^{1}/_{4}$ cups light olive oil or equal parts extra-virgin olive oil and sunflower oil
juice of $^{1}/_{2}$ lemon
1 tbsp boiling water
salt and white pepper**

First make the aïoli: peel, smash and finely chop the garlic. Put it into a bowl with the egg yolks. Start to whisk in the oil, very slowly to begin with. As it begins to thicken, season with salt and white pepper and whisk in the lemon juice. Add drops of still-hot boiled water if it gets too thick. When you have incorporated all the oil, taste and adjust the seasoning with more lemon juice, salt and pepper.

Cook the potatoes in plenty of boiling salted water. Refresh in cold water. Peel if necessary and cut in half lengthwise. Put into a bowl with the chopped herbs, tearing the sage and basil quite coarsely, and dress with olive oil to coat. Season with pepper.

Preheat the oven to 170°C / 325°F / gas 3 and put in a flat metal tin to get hot. (A non-stick Swiss roll tin is ideal.) When the oven comes up to temperature, heat a heavy, dry frying pan into which the salmon will fit. Brush the salmon all over with olive oil and season generously with salt and pepper.

Place the salmon, skin upwards, in the frying pan and sear for 60–90 seconds. Take out the hot flat tin from the oven and lay the salmon on it, skin down, and place back in the oven. It should cook for 4–5 minutes if using tail end fillet, and 7–8 minutes if using the head end. When it comes out of the oven the centre of the fillet should be slightly opaque.

Leave it to cool a little before transferring it, skin side up, to a cutting board. Remove the skin and gently scrape out the blood line, then pull away portions using a fork. It will flake and is supposed to.

Pile the salmon over the salad. Drizzle the aïoli dressing over the top and sides to serve.

Seared salmon with herbed potato salad

EGG NOODLES WITH CLAMS & CURRY MEE SAUCE

The unique flavour of this dish comes from the Penang curry powder, a subtle variation on Indian curry masalas which is more aromatic than hot. It is obtainable from Oriental markets. Chinese egg noodles can be bought in bags from the same markets, fresh or frozen. If clams are unavailable, use fresh cockles.

'I came across this dish in the early hours of one morning, eating at a roadside market in Penang with my wife's cousin. He told me that it was a favourite snack with most Malays.' MW

INGREDIENTS FOR 4

2 banana shallots (see page 66)
300ml / ¹/₂pt / 1¹/₄ cups sunflower oil
2 red chillies
bunch of coriander
32 palourde (small) clams
450g / 1lb fresh Chinese egg noodles
170g / 6oz / 1 cup beansprouts

for the curry mee sauce:
3 garlic cloves
2 banana shallots (see page 66)
5cm / 2in piece of root ginger
2 tbsp sunflower oil
1 tbsp Penang curry powder
750ml / 1¹/₄pt / 3 cups coconut milk
2 tsp nam pla Thai fish sauce

First make the sauce: peel the garlic, the 2 shallots and the ginger, and chop all of them finely. In a shallow pan, fry them gently in the oil until soft and translucent. Stir in the curry powder and cook, stirring, for 30 seconds. Add the coconut milk, turn up the heat and bring to the boil. Lower the heat to medium and bubble until well reduced, then add the fish sauce. You should have a light sauce consistency.

While the sauce is reducing, bring plenty of water to the boil in a large pan.

Peel the shallots and cut across in thin slices. Fry in the oil over a medium heat, stirring until crisp. Put on paper towels to drain. Destalk and deseed the chillies. Cut into fine julienne strips and reserve. Pick the leaves off the coriander and add to the chillies.

Put the clams in the pan of curry mee sauce, put on the lid and bubble briefly until the clams open.

Meanwhile, cook the noodles in the pan of boiling water for 2 minutes. Strain through a colander. Return to the pan with the beansprouts and toss together.

Pile these into warmed deep bowls. Divide the clams equally over them. Bring the sauce back to the boil and spoon over all. Sprinkle with shredded chilli, coriander leaves and the crispy shallots.

SEARED SQUID WITH CHINESE WATERCRESS

Use small squid tubes for this dish. Although they are not used at Quag's, frozen tubes are now available and they are very good if defrosted gently. Squid needs very little cooking – give it more than 40 seconds and you will need titanium dentures to bite through it.

'There is nothing you can substitute for tamarind, which is available from any Asian market. When you buy it, feel to make sure it is soft like putty. It is difficult to extract the pulp from old dried-out tamarind. People have been eating tamarind here for years in bottled sauces without realizing it. Choy-sum is a leaf vegetable with long stems, like a finer bok-choy, which I call Chinese watercress.' MW

INGREDIENTS FOR 4

55g / 2oz tamarind pulp
55g / 2oz / ¹/₄ cup Thai palm (or light brown) sugar
3 tbsp nam pla Thai fish sauce

juice of 1 lime
3 tbsp strong chicken stock (see page 138)
4 cleaned squid tubes
2 garlic cloves
4 banana shallots (see page 66)
2 red chillies
little sunflower oil, for frying
2 heads of small-leaf choy-sum
handful of whole coriander leaves

Make tamarind water by putting the pulp in 100ml / 3^{1}/$_{2}$fl oz of tepid water and rubbing it between your fingers until you have a thick syrup. Put through a sieve, pressing to extract as much as you can, and scraping the pulp off which will have clung to the base of the sieve.

Put this syrup with the palm sugar, fish sauce, lime juice and chicken stock in a pan and warm over a low heat, stirring until the sugar has dissolved and you have a smooth sauce. Leave to cool.

Cut down one side of each squid and open out the tube, trimming off the tail point to make a rectangle. Carefully cut a 1cm / ^{1}/$_{2}$in diamond cross-hatch on both sides, taking care not to go all the way through. Cut the rectangle into 5cm / 2in strips, pat dry with paper towels and reserve in the fridge until needed.

Peel and finely slice the garlic and the shallots. Remove the chilli stems but leave the seeds. Shred the chillies as finely as possible. Shallow-fry in 1 or 2 tablespoons of oil, stirring until all moisture has evaporated and they go crisp and golden. Remove and transfer to paper towels in a warm dry place.

Chop the leaves and stems of the choy-sum into 7.5cm / 3in lengths.

Heat a wok until smoking hot. Film with oil and immediately throw in the squid and stir and toss for 30 seconds. Add the choy-sum and toss again. Leave for 30 seconds, then remove and transfer to warmed deep bowls.

Spoon over just enough tamarind sauce to coat the squid and leaves. Finish with the crispy garnish and a scattering of whole coriander leaves.

SMOKED HADDOCK FISH CAKES

Haddock is particularly good when lightly cured and oak-smoked. The hideous bright-yellow fish that masquerades as smoked haddock in supermarkets is to be avoided at all costs. It has been dyed and is an inferior and tasteless product. Food marketers insist that bright-yellow fish sells better than the pale-golden variety, a statement that is as silly as it is sad.

'Use haddock fillets by all means. Finnan haddock, the finest smokies, are on the bone and you would have to buy a lot of this expensive fish to be able to make the dish.' MW.

INGREDIENTS FOR 8 FISH CAKES

450g / 1lb smoked haddock fillets
575ml / 1pt / 2^{1}/$_{2}$ cups milk
small bunch of flat-leaf parsley
450g / 1lb / 3 medium potatoes
115g / 4oz / 1 medium onion
1 garlic clove
bouquet garni
clarified butter or equal parts butter and sunflower oil, for frying
pepper

Pick out all the bones from the fish and also remove the skin. This is done by holding the tail end and sliding a knife between skin and flesh with the knife angled at 45 degrees to the skin.

Bring the milk to the boil in a pan, remove from the heat and drop in the haddock. Leave to stand for 5 minutes, then take out the haddock and leave to cool. Flake the flesh and chop about a quarter of the flakes finely, leaving the rest in large flakes.

Pull the leaves off the parsley, chop coarsely and add to the haddock.

Peel and dice the potatoes and onion. Peel, smash and chop the garlic. Add these to the milk with the bouquet garni and boil until the potatoes are cooked.

Remove the bouquet garni, drain the vegetables through a colander and return to the pan. Shake over a low heat to dry out any excess moisture.

Push the vegetables through a sieve and then add to the haddock and parsley. Mix thoroughly with a fork to distribute all the elements evenly. Taste and season with pepper (the fish will probably provide enough salt). When cool enough, refrigerate. This can all be done the day before use, if preferred.

Spoon out the mixture into 8 portions on a heavily

floured surface. Roll into balls with floured hands and then flatten into cakes using a palette knife.

Shallow-fry the cakes over a moderate heat in clarified butter or butter and oil. When you lay the cakes into the hot fat, leave them to cook until a crust has formed on the bottom. If you try and turn them too soon or attempt to push them around, they will break and be ruined.

Serve with rocket (arugula) leaves dressed with lemon juice or hollandaise sauce.

Pan-fried foie gras with watercress & apple

PAN-FRIED FOIE GRAS WITH WATERCRESS & APPLE

There is no reason to be scared of frying raw foie gras, the enlarged livers of corn-fed geese and ducks. It has a high fat content, some of which runs out when it hits the hot pan and has a tendency to smoke. It is fiercely expensive, but you only need 55g–85g / 2–3oz for a first-course portion since it is very rich.

'I always use duck foie gras. One can hardly use the word cheap to describe something which costs about £15 a pound, but let's just say it is less expensive than goose foie gras.' MW

INGREDIENTS FOR 4

2 Granny Smith apples

2 tbsp Calvados

2 tbsp apple juice

3^1/$_2$ tbsp red wine vinegar

100g / 3^1/$_2$oz / ^{1}/$_2$ cup sugar

bunch of watercress

4 slices of raw duck foie gras, each about 6mm / ^{1}/$_4$in thick

salt and pepper

Peel the apples, quarter them and remove the cores, then cut each quarter into 3 pieces. Put these into a bowl and pour over the Calvados and apple juice.

Boil the vinegar and sugar in a small heavy pan until the liquid colours to a dark caramel. Remove from the heat and leave to cool for 2 minutes. Then pour over the apples, stirring with a metal spoon to coat the pieces. The heat of the vinegar caramel will cook the apples slightly. Leave to cool to room temperature, then toss with the watercress.

Put a portion of apples and watercress on to each of 4 serving plates.

Put a dry, heavy frying pan over a moderate heat. When the pan is smoking-hot, season the foie gras slices with salt and pepper and sear them. Turn after 30 seconds and cook the other sides for 30 seconds more. Using a spatula, remove immediately after this minute is up, and set each slice on the plated salads. Finish with a little black pepper and serve immediately.

CHICKEN & HERB SALAD WITH ARTICHOKES

This dish treats herbs as salad leaves, a very Mediterranean approach. At Quag's, only the crown of the chicken is roasted, but it is probably easier at home to cook the whole bird. Only artichoke bottoms are used, though if you are lucky enough to get hold of whole baby artichokes before they have formed a choke then these will be even nicer.

'When preparing artichokes it is a good idea to wear rubber gloves as they discolour your hands quite dramatically.' MW

INGREDIENTS FOR 4

3 large globe artichokes

2 lemons

150ml / ^{1}/$_4$pt / 1^1/$_4$ cups olive oil

2 garlic cloves

3 crushed coriander seeds

sprig of thyme

6 spring onions (scallions)

115g / 4oz / 8 cups flat-leaf parsley

115g / 4oz / 8 cups coriander leaves

55g / 2oz / 4 cups tarragon leaves

10 basil leaves

bunch of chives

bunch of chervil

4 shallots

dash of Tabasco sauce

2 tsp Worcestershire sauce

2 tbsp tomato ketchup

1 dressed free-range chicken, weighing about 1.5kg / 3^1/$_2$lb

225g / 8oz fine French beans
5 tbsp extra-virgin olive oil
2 heads of chicory (endive)
salt and pepper

Remove the stalks from the artichokes by snapping them off cleanly. Cut the first artichoke across in half, discarding the leaves from around the base. Trim off the remaining leaves. Put the artichoke bottoms into 300ml / $^1/_2$pt / $1^1/_4$ cups of cold water, acidulated with a little juice from one of the lemons. This will help to prevent discoloration. Repeat the process with the other artichokes, adding them to the water.

Transfer the artichoke bottoms to a saucepan with 300ml / $^1/_2$pt / $1^1/_4$ cups of fresh water, the olive oil and the juice of 1 lemon. Peel and slice the garlic. Crush the coriander seeds with the flat of a knife. Add the garlic, coriander and the thyme to the pan. Bring to the boil. Reduce the heat, put on the lid and simmer for 5 minutes. Remove from the heat and leave the artichokes to cool in the liquid (which can be refrigerated and used again).

Wash, dry and trim the spring onions. Pick the leaves from the parsley and coriander, chop the remaining herbs finely and put them all in a bowl. Cut the spring onions across into thin slices and add to the bowl. Peel and thinly slice the shallots and mix in.

In another bowl, mix the Tabasco, Worcestershire sauce and ketchup. Whisk in the extra-virgin olive oil and pour this dressing over the spring onion, shallot and herb mixture. Stir and leave to infuse.

Preheat the oven to 240°C / 475°F / gas 9. Brush the chicken all over with olive oil and season generously with salt and pepper. Put it, breast side down, on a rack and roast for 30 minutes. Remove and lower the setting to 200°C / 400°F / gas 6. Turn the bird breast side up, baste with olive oil and return to the oven for 30 minutes, basting at 10-minute intervals. Remove and allow to rest for 20 minutes.

While the chicken is roasting, cook the beans. Top and tail them and blanch for 3 minutes in rapidly boiling salted water. Refresh in cold water and reserve.

Remove the breasts whole from the cooked bird. Place in a shallow dish and pour over the herb dressing while the meat is still warm. The breasts should be completely covered. Marinate at room temperature for 2 hours.

Prepare the artichokes by scraping out the fine hairs of the choke before cutting into 2cm / $^3/_4$in slices. Season lightly with salt and pepper.

Break off 12 chicory leaves and slice lengthwise into 2cm / $^3/_4$in-wide strips. Mix with the artichokes and French beans, with some of the herb dressing.

Cut the chicken breasts across into 2cm / $^3/_4$in slices.

Compose the salad on individual plates, starting with a layer of beans, one of artichoke and chicory, then some chicken slices, followed by the herb salad. Give the arrangement height. Finish by stirring the dressing and spooning it liberally over the salad.

CRISPY JAPANESE CHICKEN

There is an assumption that deep-frying demands a relatively impermeable coating like batter or egg-and-crumb to prevent the food becoming greasy. In this essentially Japanese treatment, however, the coating is made by tossing the marinated chicken in lots of flour. The residual liquid from the marinade, on the surface of the meat, binds with the flour and a lovely crunchy finish results.

INGREDIENTS FOR 4
900g / 2lb chicken breasts, skin on
3 spring onions (scallions)
3 tbsp Kikkoman soy sauce
100ml / $3^1/_2$fl oz / $^1/_2$ cup sake
15g / $^1/_2$oz / 2in piece peeled root ginger
225g / 8oz / 2 cups flour
1.5 litres / $2^1/_2$pt / $6^1/_4$ cups sunflower oil

for the dipping sauce:
8g / $^1/_4$oz / 1in piece peeled root ginger
100ml / $3^1/_2$fl oz / $^1/_2$ cup Kikkoman soy sauce

Cut the chicken into 2.5cm / 1 in strips, leaving the skin on. Trim and finely chop the spring onions and put into a bowl large enough to hold the chicken. Add the soy sauce and sake to the bowl. Grate the ginger and squeeze the moisture from it into this marinade. Put in the chicken pieces, turn to coat and cling-wrap the bowl. Marinate at room temperature for 2 hours, turning the pieces twice during this time.

Preheat the oil to 190°C / 375°F.

Drain the chicken through a colander. Put the flour in a bowl and toss the chicken pieces in it a few at a time to coat.

Fry in 4 batches until crisp and golden. Overcrowd the pan and the pieces of meat will stick together and go soggy. Each batch will take 2–3 minutes. Drain on paper towels, keeping the early batches warm while the others are cooking.

While the chicken is frying, make the dipping sauce: grate the ginger into a bowl and stir in the soy sauce.

GOATS' CHEESE & THYME SOUFFLÉ

A soufflé is one of the easiest dishes to make, yet one that never fails to impress. In this version, individual soufflés are left to cool completely, with only a brief reheating under the grill (broiler) before they come to the table. Successful soufflés stem from the confidence which comes from practice and the knowledge that the secret of success is a medium – rather than hot – oven.

'The most frequent mistake is to cook at too high a temperature, causing the soufflé to rise prematurely and this leads to collapse when it is removed from the oven. Overbeating the whites will also have the same effect.' MW

INGREDIENTS FOR 6

75g / 2¹/₂oz / 5 tbsp butter, plus more to grease the dishes
55g / 2oz / ¹/₂ cup flour
450 ml / ³/₄pt / 1²/₃ cups full-fat milk

1 tsp fresh thyme leaves (not dried)
5 size-1 (large) eggs
225g / 8oz mature goats' cheese, rind removed
200 ml / 7fl oz / ⁷/₈ cup double (heavy) cream
salt and pepper

Preheat the oven to 170°C / 325°F / gas 3. Brush 6 individual soufflé dishes with a little melted butter. Put the soufflé dishes in a roasting tin and pour water into the tin to come to halfway up the sides of the dishes.

Melt the butter in a pan and whisk in the flour to make a roux. Cook over the lowest possible heat for 3 minutes, then beat in the milk. Add the thyme, season with salt and pepper, then cook gently for 20 minutes until very thick. Remove from the heat.

Separate the eggs and beat 3 of the yolks together well. After the sauce has been cooling for 10 minutes, add these beaten egg yolks and stir to incorporate them evenly.

In a clean glass or copper bowl, whisk the egg whites until they form peaks. Stir a quarter of these into the sauce to lighten it slightly.

Dice the cheese and scatter most of it over the whisked egg whites. Then fold in the sauce, scooping and turning to achieve a light mass, but not stirring which will break down the foam needed to lift the soufflé as it cooks.

Remove the dishes from the bain-marie. Fill them almost to the rim and replace carefully. Bake for 8–10 minutes, by which time they should have risen proud above the rim of the dish. The centre should be moist, the surface golden brown and resilient to the touch. Take out of the oven and leave to cool.

Whisk the remaining egg yolks and the cream together, and season with salt and pepper. Reserve.

Run a knife round the edge of each soufflé dish and turn them out on a buttered gratin dish. Pour the liaison of the yolks and cream over and around each one and scatter the reserved diced goats' cheese over. Put in the oven preheated to 180°C / 350°F / gas 4 or under a medium grill (broiler) for 2–3 minutes. Serve at once.

ROAST PEPPER & GOATS' CHEESE TART

Peppers that have been roasted to a sweet succulence are peeled and set in a rich custard flecked with goats' cheese. The crisp thin tart shell is the same as for Quag's Spinach & Parmesan tart (see page 68).

INGREDIENTS FOR 6

5 roasted red peppers, peeled (see page 133)
8 saffron threads
1 tbsp boiling water
25cm / 10in baked tart case (see page 68)
8 eggs
350ml / 12fl oz / 1^1/2 cups whipping cream
350ml / 12fl oz / 1^1/2 cups full-fat milk
225g / 8oz mild goats' cheese
salt and pepper

Put the peppers to drain on a rack for at least an hour, to rid them of residual oil. Put the saffron in a small bowl with a tablespoon of boiling water to infuse. Preheat the oven to 150°C / 300°F / gas 2.

Put the pastry case on a baking sheet and arrange the drained peppers in a double layer in the pastry case.

Whisk the eggs, then add the saffron and its soaking liquid. Season with salt and pepper. Whisk in the cream and milk. Pour into the tart and bake for 30 minutes, when it will be three-quarters cooked. Remove and turn the oven up to its maximum setting.

Cut the goats' cheese into 1cm / ^{1}/2in dice and scatter on the top. When the oven is really hot, return the tart for 10–15 minutes to finish, removing when you have a nice gratin finish. Leave to rest for 10 minutes before cutting.

ROAST TOMATOES WITH FOCACCIA

Sweet, intensely flavoured roast tomatoes and crisp-crusted focaccia are a delicious combination. Focaccia is one of the easiest breads to make at home and a food mixer with a dough hook makes the process quick and foolproof. The dough can also, when rolled and pushed thinner, make a pizza crust. It is important to use a 14 per cent high-protein bread flour. This will be milled from 100 per cent imported Canadian flour, which has a higher protein content than domestic flours and is accordingly much more elastic, delivering a lighter bread.

'The secret of baking good focaccia my way is to have no olive oil in the mixture but to pour liberal amounts on the risen dough just before it goes into a very hot oven. We use fresh yeast in the restaurant, but dried fermipan yeast which is added with the flour is universally available and also works very well. However, you will then need to include ^{1}/2 tablespoon of olive oil and 1 teaspoon of caster sugar in the dough to get the right baked texture.' MW

INGREDIENTS FOR 4

24 warm Roast tomato halves (see page 137)
170g / 6oz rocket (arugula)
5 tbsp House dressing (see page 135)

for the focaccia:
30g / 1oz fresh yeast or ^{1}/2 a sachet (8g / ^{1}/4oz) of
    dried fermipan instant yeast plus 1tsp caster
    sugar and ^{1}/2tbsp olive oil
300ml / ^{1}/2pt / 1^1/4 cups hand-warm water
450g / 1lb / 4 cups strong white bread flour
1 tsp Maldon sea salt
olive oil, for greasing

for the focaccia dressing:
3–4 tbsp rosemary leaves

150ml / ¹/₄pt / ²/₃ cup extra-virgin olive oil
4tsp Maldon sea salt

First make the focaccia: to make by hand with fresh yeast, crumble the fresh yeast into 100ml / 3¹/₂fl oz / ¹/₂ cup of the warm water and leave for 10 minutes to froth. Put the flour on your work surface, add the yeast liquid and the rest of the warm water a spoonful at a time and mix in with your fingers, then knead for 5 minutes. Pull the dough towards you, folding over and pressing down hard with the heel of your hand. Rotate the dough a quarter turn each time you do so, repeating until you have a silky soft dough (about 5 minutes).

Form the dough into a ball, put into a bowl, cover with a cloth and leave to rise for 30–60 minutes at room temperature, ideally around 20°C / 68°F, when it

Roast tomatoes with focaccia

should have doubled or trebled in size.

If using dried fermipan yeast, put all the warm water in the bowl of a food mixer, add the dried yeast, salt, sugar and olive oil and turn on the dough hook at its lowest speed. Pour in the flour and work for 7 minutes. Turn up the speed to high and, if the dough is not smooth and elastic, add 2–3 tablespoons of warm water. Run for 1 minute and then stop. Run for longer and you risk burning out the motor of your machine.

If using a food processor, put all the dry ingredients in the bowl with the oil. Working at full speed, add the water gradually through the feeder tube. As soon as it balls, remove and continue to knead by hand on a floured surface for 5 minutes.

Transfer the dough made using dried yeast to a floured surface and form into a ball. Brush a mixing bowl with olive oil, put the dough in and brush the surface with a little more oil. Cling-wrap the top loosely, but making an airtight seal, and leave to prove in the kitchen in a cool spot for 2 hours when it will have risen above the level of the bowl. It is not good for the dough's elasticity to force this proving by putting the bowl in a very warm spot.

Whichever way you have made it and proved it, remove the dough and knock it down on a floured surface. Divide into 2. Flour the base of a shallow non-stick Swiss roll tin and roll out the dough to a thickness of 2cm / 3/4in. Lay it in the tray and finish pushing right to the edges with your fingers. Cover with towels and leave to prove again for 30–60 minutes.

Preheat the oven to 240°C / 475°F / gas 9.

Dimple the surface of the dough by pushing holes in lines with 2 fingers, then press rosemary leaves gently in between and finally pour over the olive oil. Use a brush to make sure every part is coated. Scatter on sea salt and put into the oven, being as quick as you can when opening and closing the door. Bake for 15–20 minutes, when the bread will be well risen with a crisp dark golden crust.

To serve, cut the focaccia into 3 rectangles, then cut these across diagonally to make 6 triangles. Split each triangle horizontally in half through the middle like a pitta bread and fill each with warmed oven-roast tomato halves, putting more around the edges. Toss the rocket with house dressing and put a generous handful on each plate. Dribble some olive oil on the bread, finish with a few turns of the pepper mill and serve while still warm.

NOODLES WITH CORIANDER, GINGER & CHILLI

Noodles are fantastically versatile and can be served as an unobtrusive backdrop to a sauce or act as the main feature of a dish. Here the noodles are fresh and, after brief cooking, are finished with aromatic coriander roots and leaves, shredded ginger and finely chopped hot red chilli. Ketchup manis is an Indonesian sweet soy sauce which you can buy from Asian grocers; it and nam pla – salty Thai fish sauce – complete the intriguingly complex mix of flavours.

'When you buy coriander from an Oriental market they always have roots, and these play an important role, most notably in Thai cooking. Wash these, cut them off and freeze in a zip-lock bag until needed. Coriander leaves keep well in the fridge unwashed and wrapped in newspaper. Only wash them just before use. If you wash them before fridge storage they will discolour and taint. If you can't find coriander with roots, then use the stems in place of the roots. Although most cookbooks call for the chillies to be deseeded, there is no need to do so unless you are using a lethal chilli like a habañero. You must decide for yourself how hot you want the dish to be.' MW

INGREDIENTS FOR 4
5 cm / 2 in piece of root ginger
3 garlic cloves
2 red chillies

large bunch of coriander, ideally with roots
450g / 1lb fresh Oriental noodles
6 spring onions (scallions)
3 tbsp sunflower oil
2 tbsp ketchup manis
1/2 tbsp nam pla Thai fish sauce

Put a large pan of unsalted water to boil. Peel and chop the ginger; peel, smash and chop the garlic. Destalk the chillies and then cut them across into thin rings.

Pull the leaves from the coriander and finely chop the roots (or stems if you haven't got roots).

Boil the noodles for 2–3 minutes, until just tender. They should be *al dente*. Drain and reserve. Top and tail the spring onions, slice finely and reserve.

Put the oil into a heavy, hot frying pan or wok and add the ginger, coriander roots or stems and the garlic. Cook over a high heat, stirring and tossing, for 1 minute. Add the ketchup manis and continue to stir-fry for another minute.

Add the noodles to the pan and toss to coat, then add the spring onions. Lastly, add 2 tablespoons of coriander leaves and the fish sauce.

Toss once more and serve at once in warmed deep bowls, scattered with the chilli rings and remaining coriander leaves.

BUTTERNUT SQUASH SOUP WITH SMOKED BACON & PARSLEY

Squash are edible gourds and have long been associated with American cooking, though they also feature extensively in the cuisine of south-western France. Recently, with the popularity of the smaller butternut squash, more people have come to enjoy them.

'This soup has a lovely, burnt-orange colour and takes on a delicate smokiness from the bacon. This dish is an Australian staple that crops up everywhere.' MW

INGREDIENTS FOR 4

1kg / 2 1/4lb butternut squash
1/2 onion
2 garlic cloves
225g / 8oz smoked streaky (thick-sliced) bacon
100g / 3 1/2oz / 7 tbsp unsalted butter
1 litre / 1 3/4pt / 4 1/3 cups chicken stock
   (see page 138)
150ml / 1/4pt / 2/3 cup milk
5 tbsp chopped flat-leaf parsley
100ml / 3 1/2fl oz / 1/2 cup double (heavy) cream, plus
   more to garnish
2 slices of white bread
salt and pepper

Peel the squash with a potato peeler. Cut in half, deseed and chop the flesh coarsely. Peel the onion and garlic and chop both coarsely.

Cut the bacon into lardon strips and cook gently in a dry frying pan until nearly crisp and the fat has run. Transfer the bacon to a plate and reserve. Keep the pan with the fat in it to cook the croûtons later.

Put the butter in a large saucepan together with the squash, onion and garlic and sweat gently until soft. Add the bacon, pour in the stock and bring to the boil. Then lower the heat and simmer for 20 minutes.

Add the milk and three-quarters of the chopped parsley, then season with salt and pepper. Raise the heat, bubble briskly and remove from the stove.

In a liquidizer or processor, purée the soup in batches, returning each to the pan. Bring back to a simmer and stir in the cream. Season, to taste.

Make the croûtons: cut the crusts off the bread and cut into 1cm / 1/2in dice. Fry until crisp in the bacon fat, adding a little butter to the pan if required.

Ladle the soup into bowls and garnish with a swirl of cream, the croûtons and the remaining parsley.

FIELD MUSHROOMS ON TOAST

There is an understandable degree of confusion about mushrooms; not just those which more and more people seek out in the wild, but those we buy in shops and supermarkets – the majority of which are cultivated. The true field mushroom is Agaricus campestris. *If you know where to gather them, lucky you. If not, buy the largest cultivated flat-cap mushrooms you can find –* Agaricus bisporus – *which have the best flavour.*

INGREDIENTS FOR 4

900g / 2lb flat-cap mushrooms
125ml / 4fl oz / $\frac{1}{2}$ cup extra-virgin olive oil
4 thick slices of crusty white bread (not pre-sliced)
2 large garlic cloves
2 tbsp chopped flat-leaf parsley
salt and pepper

Preheat a moderate grill (broiler). Wipe the mushrooms and remove the stems. Keep these to add to a stock. Place the caps, stalk ends up, on a baking tray. Brush with olive oil, then sprinkle with salt and pepper.

Put under the grill and cook slowly. They are done when the undersides are very dark and drops of moisture start to form at the stem point. Remove and cool.

Heat a ridged grill pan, from underneath. Brush both sides of the bread with olive oil. Place the slices on the hot pan for 10 seconds. Turn, and cook the other side for a further 10 seconds.

Cut the mushrooms into 1cm / $\frac{1}{2}$in slices. Peel, smash and chop the garlic finely.

Put a frying pan over a moderate heat. Add 3 tablespoons of olive oil and then the chopped garlic. Sauté briefly, until soft but not coloured – perhaps 30 seconds, no more (take the garlic too far and it will become bitter). Add the mushrooms and stir and toss until hot. Add the chopped parsley and toss to mix in. Turn off the heat but leave the mushrooms in the pan.

Transfer the toasts to large warmed plates. Mound the mushrooms on top and serve at once.

Field mushrooms on toast

ARTICHOKE & PARSLEY SOUP

Just why Jerusalem artichokes are so called is not clear, for they originate from North America, are a knobbly thick-skinned root vegetable and have no relationship with globe artichokes which are essentially thistles. The French call this soup purée de topinambours.

'How much artichoke you have to work with after peeling will depend on how knobbly they are to start with. The smoother they are, the less waste. Fortunately they are not expensive, so you can always buy an extra 450g / 1lb without flinching. Artichoke soup is usually made with a light chicken stock base, but the Quag's version uses a fine full-flavoured vegetable stock.' MW

INGREDIENTS FOR 6

900g / 2lb Jerusalem artichokes
1 onion
1 garlic clove
3 tbsp olive oil
170g / 6oz / 1 medium potato
2 shallots
small bunch of flat-leaf parsley
100ml / 3$\frac{1}{2}$fl oz / $\frac{1}{2}$ cup double (heavy) cream
salt and pepper

for the vegetable stock:
225g / 8oz / 2 medium onions
1 leek
$\frac{1}{2}$ fennel bulb
1 carrot
1 celery stick
3 tbsp olive oil
$\frac{1}{4}$ English cabbage
few sprigs of flat-leaf parsley including stalks
handful of chives
6 basil leaves
1 star anise
salt and 10 black peppercorns, crushed

First make the stock: trim all the vegetables except the cabbage and cut them into 2.5cm / 1in pieces. Put the olive oil in a casserole, add the chopped vegetables, cover with a lid and sweat over a low heat, until softened and translucent. Be careful not to let the vegetables colour. Chop the cabbage finely and add together with the herbs, star anise, salt and peppercorns. Pour over 2 litres / 3½pts / 8¾ cups of cold water, turn up the heat and bring to the boil. Skim, lower the heat and bubble with the lid off for 10–15 minutes, skimming from time to time. Take off the heat and allow to cool, then pass through a fine sieve. Squeeze down on the vegetables with a wooden spoon to extract all the juices. The stock produced should be quite clear but have a good flavour. Return to a clean saucepan and heat gently.

To make the soup: trim off any black bits from the artichokes, peel them and chop into 2.5cm / 1in pieces. Peel the onion and dice. Peel, smash and chop the garlic. Put them all into a casserole with the olive oil and sweat over a low heat until translucent. Peel the potatoes, dice and add to the pot. Pour over the hot stock, season with salt and pepper and bring to the boil. Lower the heat to a gentle bubble and cook for 20 minutes, until all the ingredients are cooked.

Use a slotted spoon to remove some pieces of artichoke to put into soup bowls. Liquidize the rest in a blender or processor and pass through a conical strainer into a clean saucepan. Keep hot over low heat.

To finish: peel the shallots and shave into the thinnest possible slices. Destalk the parsley. Stir the double cream into the soup. Into each of 6 warmed soup plates, put some crushed artichoke pieces, a tablespoon of parsley leaves and some shallot. Ladle the soup over to cover completely and finish with a turn or two of ground pepper.

DUCK SOUP WITH NOODLES AND CORIANDER

The Chinese can claim to be the best duck cooks in the world, with Cantonese roast duck and Peking duck among their finest culinary expressions. Both these preparations involve special ovens and techniques, and are dishes which Chinese people would not tend to cook at home, preferring to go to restaurants which produce them perfectly and on a large scale. Duck soup is more forgiving and equally delicious, and in this treatment is distinguished by the addition of Thai fish sauce to the broth.

> *'Although it is called a soup, this can be a main course and in the Far East would always be served as one. For those who like some fire to cut the richness of the duck, provide thinly sliced hot red chillies, but offer them on a separate plate.'* MW

INGREDIENTS FOR 4 (POSSIBLY MORE)
- **1 oven-ready duck, weighing about 1.5kg / 3½lb**
- **5cm / 2in piece of root ginger**
- **2 carrots**
- **1 leek**
- **1 onion**
- **1 celery stick**
- **6 star anise**
- **15–20 black peppercorns**
- **1 tbsp nam pla Thai fish sauce**
- **2 tbsp dark sesame oil**
- **1 large bunch of coriander, including roots**
- **450g / 1lb Oriental 'no-cook' egg noodles**
- **8 spring onions (scallions)**
- **3–4 hot red chillies (optional)**
- **salt**

Preheat the oven to 220°C / 425°F / gas 7. Pull out any lumps of fat from inside the duck and rub the skin lightly with salt. Place on a roasting rack, breast side down over a roasting pan and roast for 15 minutes. Turn it breast side up, lower the temperature to 200°C / 400°F / gas 6 and continue to cook for a further 1 hour. Remove from the oven and leave to rest and cool on the rack. Cut the leg, thigh and breast meat from the bird, removing the breasts in single pieces.

Chop the carcass into 4 pieces and put in a large pan. Cover with 4 litres / 7 pints / 8³/4 pints of cold water and bring to the boil. While the water is heating, peel and cut the ginger into thin slices, peel the carrots, clean and trim the leek, and top and tail the onion (do not peel) and the celery. Then chop them all coarsely and reserve. When the water boils, skim off the scum and lower the heat to a simmer. Add the chopped vegetables, the ginger, star anise and peppercorns. Remove the meat from the duck thighs and legs and add the bones to the pot. Simmer for 4–5 hours, skimming at regular intervals.

The stock should be reduced by about half and will be clear and jewel-bright. Pass it through a fine sieve into a clean saucepan. Bring back to the boil, lower the heat to a simmer and add the fish sauce and sesame oil.

Pick off the leaves from the coriander and reserve. Clean and chop the stems and roots, add them to the stock and simmer for 15 minutes.

Just before the stock will be ready, reconstitute the noodles following the packet instructions. (This usually involves pouring boiling water over them and leaving them to soak for 3–4 minutes.)

Cut the duck meat into 1 cm / ¹/2 in slices and thinly slice the spring onions and chillies. Drain the noodles and place them in 4 deep bowls. Scatter with the spring onion and chillies, then share out the duck meat, arranging this on top. Ladle over the broth and finally scatter over the coriander leaves.

Duck soup with noodles and coriander

MAIN COURSES

COOKING AND PREPARING CRABS AND LOBSTERS

Crabs and lobsters are things that people rarely cook and prepare at home, and this is something of a pity. Cooking simply involves boiling in heavily salted water, while preparation is principally a case of getting the meat from the shells. This is time-consuming rather than difficult, and an activity where practice does indeed make perfect.

Start with a crab, which is cheaper. You will be cooking it in its live state. Be brave and look him in the eye, remembering that a watery grave is entirely appropriate for a sea creature. If it is not long from the sea a crab can move with surprising speed so when picking it up do so with conviction, gripping the shell from behind. Drop one and it will shed a claw out of sheer spite.

The cooking water should be as salty as the sea, a salinity equivalent achieved by adding 140g / 5oz / ½ cup salt to every 5 litres / 9 pints of water. The size of the crab or crabs will determine the size of the pot and the amount of water. Bring this to the boil and drop the crab in. A crab can weigh from 550g / 1¼lb upwards. A 600g / 1lb 6oz specimen will take 15 minutes from returning to the boil, while one weighing up to 900g / 2lb will take 20 minutes. Between 900g / 2lb and 1.5 kg / 3½lb, they will take 25 minutes. Over that, no matter how big, it will take no more than 30 minutes. A boil does not mean a fast rolling boil, but a simmer with just an occasional bubble breaking the surface. When cooked, drain and let cool.

Once the crab is cool, put it on its back and twist off the claws and legs. Crack the claws open with a hammer or the back of a heavy knife. Don't hit it so hard it shatters and damages the flesh. Pull away the shell and extract the flesh. A gentle but firm pull will bring away not only the claw meat but also the tip concealed inside the pincer. Repeat with the remaining claw segments, then deal with the legs, which have a much softer shell.

Give the tail flap a knock to loosen it, before using a knife or screwdriver to lever out the underside panel to which the legs were attached. As you lift it up it will pull away the bony central section. Reserve this as it contains most of the white meat.

Behind the mouth you will find the stomach sac and bits. Throw these away, then use a small spoon to scrape out the brown flesh from the outer sections of the shell. Remove the translucent gills (dead men's fingers) that are curled over the bony central section. Cut down and through this in a 'V' to give you four accessible planes and use a thin skewer to extract all the meat concealed in the little pockets and channels. Turn it the other way up and scrape out the remaining white flesh from the leg sockets.

You now have the prime white and red claw meat, ivory shell meat and brown meat (including the liver) from the shell extremities.

Lobsters are cooked in exactly the same way as crab, but take slightly less time. A 550g / 1¼lb lobster will take 13 minutes, a 675g / 1½lb lobster 15 minutes and one up to 1.1kg / 2½lb 20 minutes. Over that weight, allow an extra 5 minutes per 450g / 1lb.

Cutting a lobster in half demands commitment in the stroke. If you are right-handed, position the lobster on its belly and with the head pointing to the right. With a heavy, pointed and sharp-bladed knife, insert the point where the carapace joins the tail section, then drive down and cut towards the head, slamming down with the flat of your hand on the knife to cut cleanly through the shell. Turn the lobster, reinsert the knife in the same central line and cut through to the tail.

'The lobster is easier to deal with than the crab. Only the gravel sac and intestinal tract towards the mouth are inedible. The green tomalley in the carapace is delicious and the tail meat lifts out in one piece. Never throw away crab or lobster shells. Use them to make stock, which can be reduced and frozen, or crustacea oil as described on page 139.' MW

SCALLOPS WITH ROAST TOMATOES, THYME & GARLIC

Scallops hardly need any cooking if their sweet and expensive flesh is not to become unpleasantly chewy. The simplest treatment shows them in their best light and in this dish they are briefly seared and served with roast tomatoes, thyme and garlic.

Ask your fishmonger to open and clean the scallops for you as this is quite a tricky task. Never use frozen scallops; their delicate meat is ruined and you end up paying a lot of money for watery and tasteless rubber discs. Far better to make this recipe with fillets of sea bream or red mullet.

'There is a current fashion for removing the roes which seems to me nonsensical, putting appearance before flavour. I think the roes are one of the nicest things about them.' MW

INGREDIENTS FOR 4

16 fresh large scallops with roes, if possible
2 tbsp olive oil
85g / 3oz / 6 tbsp unsalted butter
2 garlic cloves, peeled and chopped
1 tbsp fresh thyme leaves
juice of 1 lemon
8 Roast tomato halves (see page 137)
salt and pepper

Scallops with roast tomatoes, thyme & garlic

Season the scallops lightly with salt and pepper. Preheat a heavy frying pan until smoking hot. Add the olive oil, put the scallops in and sear for 1–2 minutes. Do not push them or prod them. Turn carefully with a palette knife or spatula and sear the other side for a further 1–2 minutes. The precise time will depend on the size of the scallops, but they should be only just cooked. Remove from the pan and keep warm.

Put the butter in the pan and as it starts to foam add the garlic and thyme. Shake the pan and as it starts to brown add the lemon juice. Remove from the heat.

Place 2 halves of roast tomato in the centre of the plate, arrange the scallops around them and pour over the garlic lemon butter.

OLIVE-OIL-ROASTED CRAYFISH

Perth, Australia's westernmost seaport, looks inland across a rich belt of sheep-farming country. It is hot and arid, so farmers dig out huge holes in the ground and dam them to capture the infrequent rains, making water-holes for the sheep. They then seed these water-holes with yabbies, freshwater crayfish that have the dual advantage of keeping the water clean and oxygenated while providing the 'cockies' – as the farmers are called locally – with a welcome and delicious shellfish crop. Others also have an interest in the small and delicious crustacea, which have larger claws and a higher meat yield than their European counterpart. Birds hover, ever-ready to scoop the crayfish from the shallows.

'When available I buy in 120kg / 265lb of live yabbies a week from Perth. They are hardy and resilient and, if kept cool and damp, happily survive two weeks in polystyrene boxes without deterioration. They feature widely on the menu: in the crayfish cocktail, on the Plateau de Fruits de Mer *and, as here, simply roasted with olive oil and herbs.'* MW

INGREDIENTS FOR 4

20 freshwater crayfish
3 tbsp olive oil
2 lemons, to serve
2 bunches of watercress, to serve
salt and pepper

for the dressing:
1 tbsp finely chopped chervil
1 tbsp finely chopped tarragon
1 tbsp finely chopped fennel leaves
1 tbsp finely chopped parsley
4 tbsp extra-virgin olive oil
black pepper

Put all the herbs for the dressing to infuse in the extra-virgin olive oil with 2 teaspoons of coarsely milled black pepper. Preheat the oven to 240°C / 475°F / gas 9.

Split the crayfish down the back, inserting the knife in the centre at the point where the carapace meets the flexible tail section, and remove the intestinal thread running the length of the body. Crack the claws with the back of a heavy knife. Season with salt and pepper.

Put over a medium heat a heavy pan that will go in the oven and is large enough to hold the crayfish in a single layer. When very hot, swirl in the olive oil and immediately place the crayfish in the pan, flesh side down. After 30 seconds, shake and turn them with tongs until they begin to blush red. Then transfer to the oven.

Give them 3–4 minutes only in the oven and remove when they are bright red.

Put them on warmed plates, flesh side up, and spoon over the herb dressing. Finish the plates with a half lemon and a handful of watercress.

COD & LEEK GRATIN

This is a superior fish pie, combining the richness of a gratin Dauphinoise with mouthfuls of tender cod.

'I once ate in a restaurant in Berne which only served gratins. This one was accompanied by delicious local wine and country bread.' MW

INGREDIENTS FOR 4
    450g / 1lb leeks
    1 garlic clove
    55g / 2oz / 4 tbsp unsalted butter
    900g / 2lb potatoes, peeled
    575ml / 1pt / 2$^1/_2$ cups double (heavy) cream
    $^1/_2$ nutmeg, grated
    675g / 1$^1/_2$lb boneless, skinned cod fillet
    85g / 3oz Emmenthal cheese, grated
    30g / 1oz Parmesan, grated
    salt and pepper

Top, tail, trim and wash the leeks to remove any dirt. Cut across into 1cm / $^1/_2$in rings. Peel, smash and chop the garlic. Put the leeks and garlic in a pan with the butter and sweat gently for 3–4 minutes until soft. Season with salt and reserve.

Preheat the oven to 180°C / 350°F / gas 4.

Slice the potatoes thinly on a mandoline. Wash, wrap in a cloth and wring dry. Put in a bowl with the cream. Season with salt, pepper and nutmeg, stir together and reserve.

Cut the cod into chunks and butter a gratin dish. Spoon half the potato cream mixture in the base. Distribute chunks of cod evenly on top. Cover with the leek and garlic mixture, then with the grated Emmenthal. Lay on the remaining potatoes and pour over the rest of the cream. Sprinkle the top with Parmesan and bake for 45 minutes.

Flash briefly under the grill (broiler) and serve from the dish at the table with a basket of crusty white bread.

ROAST HALIBUT WITH SPICED LENTILS & CORIANDER

Lentilles de Puy are the finest lentils in the world, dark green and with a marvellous flavour, and take less cooking than other lentils. They should be cooked until only just done and never to a porridge.

'This is one of those East-meets-West dishes, I suppose. The halibut is a very English fish, the lentils are French and the spicing is Southeast, Asian. They all go together brilliantly.' MW

INGREDIENTS FOR 4
    2 tomatoes
    4 garlic cloves
    4 shallots
    2 fresh hot red chillies
    4 tbsp sunflower oil
    2 whole cardamom pods
    1 star anise
    1 tsp turmeric
    350g / 12oz / 1$^3/_4$ cups Puy lentils
    1 litre / 1$^3/_4$pt / 4$^1/_3$ cups fish stock
    150ml / $^1/_4$pt / $^2/_3$ cup double (heavy) cream
    juice of 1 lemon
    3 tbsp nam pla Thai fish sauce
    3 red onions
    55g / 2oz / 4 tbsp butter
    55g / 2oz / 4 cups coriander
    900g / 2lb boneless, skinless halibut fillet
    salt and pepper

Blanch the tomatoes in boiling water for 30 seconds, refresh in cold water and peel. Dice and reserve. Peel, smash and chop the garlic, peel and dice the shallots and shred the chillies.

Put the oil in a pan over a low heat, add the chopped vegetables, the whole cardamom pods, star anise and the turmeric and sweat them, stirring, for 2–3 minutes. Add the lentils, stir and pour in the fish stock.

Bring to the boil, lower the heat, and simmer for 12–15 minutes by which time the lentils should be just cooked. Remove the cardamom pods and discard. Stir in the lemon juice, cream and fish sauce, taste, season with salt and pepper, taste again, and keep warm over the lowest heat.

Cut the onions in half, then across into the thinnest slices you can manage. Sweat in the butter until soft and transparent. About 4 minutes.

Return the lentils to a low heat to warm through. Pick the leaves from the coriander and reserve.

Cut the halibut into four neat, rectangular portions. Put a dry frying pan over a medium flame to get very hot and heat the grill (broiler). Brush the fish steaks with oil, then season with salt and pepper and lay them in the pan. After 60 seconds transfer the pan under the grill (broiler) for 3 minutes. Remove.

Stir half the coriander into the onions and half into the lentils. Put a ladle of lentils and sauce on each heated plate. Lay a halibut steak on top and finish with a spoonful of wilted onions and coriander on the fish.

DEEP FRIED SKATE FILLETS IN YEAST BATTER

Skate on the bone is a difficult fish to deep fry since it is very large and uneven in shape and thickness. Fillets of skate, however, are ideal. The yeast batter is very English, though not widely used today, and delivers an excellent, crisp result. Cut the chips (fries) quite thick, say 6cm x 2cm (2^1/2 x ^{3}/4 in).

If you can get hold of fresh yeast then use it, but dried yeast will work efficiently enough.

INGREDIENTS FOR 4
**900g / 2lb floury (Idaho-type) potatoes
2 litres / 3^1/2pts / 9 cups (approx) sunflower oil for
 deep frying
4 x 170g / 6oz skate fillets
225g / 8oz / 2 cups strong plain (all-purpose) flour
large bunch of watercress, to serve
2 lemons, to serve**

for the yeast batter:
**350ml / 12fl oz / 1^1/2 cups milk
30g / 2oz fresh yeast
or
1 sachet fermipan dried yeast
55g / 2oz / ^{1}/2 cup flour, sifted
salt and pepper**

for the tartare sauce:
**55g / 2oz / ^{1}/4 cup small gherkins
30g / 1oz / 2 tbsp capers
1 tbsp chives
1 tbsp chopped parsley
1 tbsp chopped chervil
300ml / ^{1}/2pt / 1^1/4 cups thick mayonnaise**

Make the yeast batter. Heat the milk to blood temperature and pour into a large bowl as it will rise in a spectacular way. Whisk in the yeast, then the sifted flour, until smooth. Season with salt and pepper. Cover the bowl with cling-film and leave to prove for 1 hour.

Make the tartare sauce: rinse the gherkins and capers, dry and chop finely. Cut the chives small. Put them, together with the parsley and chervil, in a bowl and stir in mayonnaise to make a thick sauce. Season to taste, then transfer to a sauce boat.

Peel the potatoes and cut into chips (fries). Put into cold water for 10 minutes to remove surface starch, drain through a colander and pat dry.

Preheat sunflower oil in an electric fryer to 190°C / 375°F. Never deep fry at a depth of more than half the pan and use one with a lid which can be put on in the event of fire. Always gauge the temperature with a thermometer. Blanch the chips (fries) in batches for 5 minutes, remove and reserve.

Dip the fillets in the flour then into the batter, shaking to allow excess to drop back into the bowl. Fry until crisp and golden brown, turning once. This will take about 4 minutes. Put to drain on paper towels.

Plunge the chips (fries) back in the basket to crisp for about 60 seconds. Serve the skate and chips with a little watercress and some lemon on each plate. Put the tartare sauce in a bowl before placing on the table for people to help themselves.

Roast cod with clams

ROAST COD WITH CLAMS

Roast cod and clams look stunning on the plate and are delicious together. Palourdes are the preferred clams for this dish, but any other small clam – like clovisse, Venus or carpet shell – could be substituted. The clams exude a lot of delicious salty juice when they are cooked in the pan with olive oil and this, with the garlic and parsley, makes all the sauce needed. If you can't get clams use cockles or small mussels of a uniform size.

INGREDIENTS FOR 4

4 tbsp extra-virgin olive oil
4 cod fillets, each weighing about 200g / 7oz
1 garlic clove
30–40 clams
1 tbsp chopped flat-leaf parsley
salt and pepper

Preheat the oven to its maximum setting.

Using one-quarter of the oil, brush the cod portions top and bottom and season lightly with salt and pepper.

Peel, smash and finely chop the garlic.

Heat a heavy frying pan in which all 4 pieces of cod will fit comfortably and which can go straight from the hob (stove top) into the oven. When smoking hot, lay the cod in it, skin side down, until this takes on a good colour – but be careful not to burn it.

Immediately the skin is golden brown, move the pan into the oven to finish, which will take about 4 minutes.

While the fish is cooking, put a lidded saucepan on a medium heat. Put in the remaining olive oil and stir in the garlic. Leave for 10 seconds, then add the clams. Put the lid on and shake. Steam briefly until the clams open (about 60 seconds). As soon as they do, remove from the heat, add the chopped parsley and some milled pepper, then stir all together.

Put the cod on warmed serving plates, skin side up. Spoon the clams around each and dress with the parsley and oil mixture.

ROAST COD WITH ARTICHOKE MASH

Cod is today enjoying enormous popularity in restaurants, almost certainly for the wrong reasons. Overfishing is causing prices to soar, and when we have to pay more for something it often seems that our appreciation of its value changes.

The fish is served here simply dressed with a little lemon and oil. Restaurant ovens are capable of delivering 300°C, far in excess of the temperature a domestic cooker can achieve. However, some domestic ovens have an internal grill (broiler) element that can be combined with convection heating. Here a temperature of 240°C / 475°F will do the job, since effectively it has been boosted by fan distribution of the hot air. A lower temperature does not preclude roasting cod fillet, but there is a much greater risk of overcooking and drying the fish. In a domestic context it is therefore preferable to use a combined cooking technique, where the fish is started skin side down in a hot dry pan and then finished off under a grill (broiler).

'Cod has always been a splendid fish at any price, with moist large flakes and fillets from which all bones are easily removed. It is the cook's dream ingredient, for its delicate flavour lends itself readily to many interpretations. Artichoke mash makes a lovely accompaniment to roast cod. This is made from Jerusalem artichokes, the dull appearance of which belies their intense and aromatic flavour.' MW

INGREDIENTS FOR 4
900 g / 2lb piece of cod fillet
1–2 tbsp olive oil
extra-virgin olive oil, to dress
2 lemons, to serve
bunch of watercress, to serve
salt and pepper

for the artichoke mash:
750 g / 1³/₄lb Jerusalem artichokes
150 ml / ¹/₄pt / ²/₃ cup double (heavy) cream
3 tbsp chopped flat-leaf parsley
salt and pepper

Put on a pan of salted water to boil for the artichokes. If you have an oven that will achieve 270°C / 518°F, preheat to maximum, otherwise, preheat an overhead grill (broiler).

Remove all the pin bones from the fish, then cut the cod fillet into 4 neat pieces about 200g / 7oz each, leaving the skin on. Brush the skin with olive oil and season top and bottom with salt and pepper.

Peel the artichokes and boil in the water for 15–20 minutes until done. Drain through a colander. Return to the hot pan over a low heat and shake for a few seconds until completely dry.

Mash with a potato masher until smooth, but do not take it too far – this is not supposed to be a fine purée. Beat in the cream and chopped parsley. Taste and season with salt and pepper. Keep warm.

If you are using the oven method, put to heat on the hob (stove top) a heavy dry pan that will go in the oven.

(A Le Creuset pan is perfect for this job.) It should be large enough to hold the fillets in one layer. When the pan is very hot, lay the cod fillets in it, skin side down and cook for 2–3 minutes. At this point the skin should be crisp and mottled with brown spots. Put the fillets into the oven for a further 2–3 minutes.

If your oven is not capable of reaching the high temperature demanded, preheat an overhead grill (broiler). Start the cod cooking in the pan as above, but finish under the grill (broiler) for 2–3 minutes.

As soon as they are cooked, carefully transfer the fillets to warmed plates, skin side up, and dribble with a little extra-virgin olive oil. Place a scoop of artichoke mash to one side and a half lemon and bunch of water-cress on each plate. Serve at once.

GRILLED SKATE WITH SAUCE GRIBICHE

Skate is a member of the ray family, a delicious but largely unappreciated fish characterized by its fan of gelatinous bones on which the sweet white flesh resides in pretty scalloped steaks – making it easy to fillet into neat portions. It is mostly eaten in the south of England, battered, with chips (fries), and is hardly eaten at all in the north of the country and Scotland.

There is an odd and enduring piece of received wisdom about skate, that when very fresh the fish smells of ammonia. The opposite is true. A strong whiff of ammonia means the fish has been dead for an unacceptably long time. If it smells, do not accept it. The amount of fish specified sounds a lot, but the bone-to-flesh ratio is higher than with most fish.

'Pan-fried skate is classically sauced with black butter, a misnomer for lightly browned butter. Black butter would be burnt and bitter. Sauce gribiche is one of the finest cold sauces of the French kitchen: forceful, distinctive, and the perfect foil for the rich skate. It makes an excellent alternative to the sauce tartare more commonly served with fried fish dishes.' MW

INGREDIENTS FOR 4
4 skate wings, each weighing about 450g / 1lb
olive oil, for brushing
2 lemons

Grilled skate with sauce gribiche

for the sauce gribiche:

2 hard-boiled eggs, separated
2 raw egg yolks
2 tbsp white wine vinegar
300 ml / ½ pt / 1¼ cups olive oil
3 tbsp sunflower oil
2 tsp chopped chervil
1 tsp chopped tarragon
1 tbsp chopped capers
3 tbsp chopped gherkins
2 tsp Dijon mustard
salt and pepper

Make the sauce gribiche: put the yolks of the cooked eggs in a bowl and mash with a fork. Stir in the raw egg yolks, season with salt and pepper, then start to beat in some of the vinegar. Add the oils a few teaspoons at a time, as for making mayonnaise, alternating with drips of vinegar as it thickens. If it gets too thick, thin with teaspoons of warm water. You should have a smooth thick yellow sauce by the time all the oil and vinegar have been incorporated.

Chop the white of one boiled egg and add, then stir in the chopped herbs, capers, gherkins and mustard. Taste and season if needed. Cling-wrap and refrigerate. This can be done the day before.

Each skate wing fans down from a solid pinkish main bone. Using a small sharp knife, follow the edge of this bone along its length, sliding and cutting with the knife angled downwards to the secondary bones. Lift the flesh away and work to the tip, sliding and cutting to lift the flesh away in a neat fillet. One side will be larger than the other and 2 fillets from 1 wing will make a single portion.

You can either sear the fillets in a hot frying pan or cook on a ridged grill pan. While the latter gives a more pleasing presentation, it is not so easy as the skate has a tendency to stick and tear between the ridges. You can also use an overhead grill (broiler). Whichever method you choose, remember that the skate fillets are very thin and take almost no cooking. First brush the fillets with olive oil and season with salt and pepper, then give them no more than 2 minutes on each side.

Serve the sauce gribiche at room temperature in a sauce-boat beside a bowl of chips (fries) or mashed potatoes. Put a half lemon on each plate. For those who feel cheated without a green vegetable, blanched buttery spinach combines well with everything else.

SWORDFISH WITH SALSA CRUDA & LIME

Salsas are among Mexico's nicest culinary exports and almost always include ripe tomatoes and onion in the mix, but the important thing is to make them fresh. To allow all the flavours to amalgamate you should always leave them to stand for an hour before serving. However, as all the ingredients are raw, that freshness and clean taste deteriorate with oxidization, so they should really be eaten the same day.

Swordfish are increasingly available from our better fishmongers and some supermarkets. You could use steaks of any other meaty fish, like tuna or salmon.

'This dish is typical of western Australian restaurants, with simple grilling and accompanying salsa. Salsas make lovely cold sauces for many cooked dishes. Spice them up with hot chilli and substitute coriander for basil and you have an excellent dip to serve with corn chips.' MW

INGREDIENTS FOR 4

450g / 1lb very ripe red plum tomatoes
1 red onion
12 basil leaves
1 garlic clove, peeled, smashed and finely chopped
juice of 1 lime
150ml / ¼pt / ⅔ cup extra-virgin olive oil, plus
  more for brushing
4 swordfish steaks, each weighing about 225g / 8oz
salt and pepper

Put the tomatoes into a bowl and pour boiling water over them to cover. Leave for 10–15 seconds, refresh in cold water and peel. Cut into 5mm / ¼in dice and put into a bowl.

Peel and dice the onion to the same size and add. Finely chop the basil and stir in with the garlic. Season with a little salt and pepper, then pour over the lime juice and olive oil. Stir together and leave for an hour. Stir again before serving.

Preheat a very hot grill (broiler). Brush the fish with a little oil. Season with salt and pepper and grill for 3 minutes on each side. Serve with the salsa on the side.

Glazed mackerel with soy & ginger

GLAZED MACKEREL WITH SOY & GINGER

This very Japanese treatment is appropriate for a fish which is more honoured in that country than it is here. Ask your fishmonger to fillet two large mackerel for you and remove the pin bones, giving you four fillets. An oily fish, mackerel is perfect for grilling and takes very little cooking. The glaze is based on teriyaki, the Japanese barbecue sauce.

The rice used here is the round-grained glutinous rice that you can now buy in small packets in super-

markets, but it really is worth going to an Oriental market and buying a big bag. The savings in doing so are huge.

'Electric rice steamers are inexpensive and are used universally throughout Southeast Asia, but the method given below will work as long as you follow the instructions to the letter.' MW

INGREDIENTS FOR 4

2 cm / ³/₄in piece of peeled root ginger
2 limes
5 tbsp Kikkoman soy sauce
4 tbsp mirin
3 tbsp sake
600g / 1lb 6oz / 3 cups Japanese rice
4 mackerel fillets, each weighing about 200g / 7oz

Grate the peeled ginger over a piece of butter muslin (cheesecloth). Squeeze this into a bowl to extract the juice. Add the juice of 1 of the limes and reserve.

Bring the soy sauce, mirin and sake to a boil in a small saucepan and immediately remove from the heat. Then allow to cool before adding to the lime juice and ginger to make the glaze.

Put the precisely measured rice in a saucepan that has a tight-fitting lid with 400ml / 14fl oz / 1³/₄ cups of water and bring to the boil. As soon as it boils, cover tightly, lower the heat to a bare simmer and cook for 15 minutes. After this time, turn off the heat and leave with the lid on for a further 15 minutes. At no time remove the lid until the moment of service.

Preheat an overhead grill (broiler) to medium. Brush the fish fillets all over with the glaze and put under the grill (broiler), skin side up. Cook for 3 minutes, brushing more glaze on while it grills. Turn and cook the other side, again brushing on more glaze. When done, the fillets will be a rich dark-brown colour.

Serve the glazed mackerel on warmed plates with the plain steamed fragrant rice and the remaining lime cut into wedges.

RED MULLET WITH POTATOES & BLACK OLIVES

Red mullet is actually pink, with lovely firm white flesh that pulls apart in large moist flakes when cooked. The treatment in this recipe is very Mediterranean.

'Red mullet are quite small fish, not usually running above 450g / 1lb. They are not difficult fish to fillet, but by all means get your fishmonger to do the job for you. Even so, always check for pin bones by running your fingertips from the head end of the fillet towards the tail. Use a pair of strong tweezers to pull out any bones that you find. It is easiest done by pulling in the same direction as the grain of the flesh.' MW

INGREDIENTS FOR 2

4 red mullet fillets, skin on, each about 115g / 4oz
1 onion
1 garlic clove
3 ripe plum tomatoes
10 new potatoes
12 black olives
1 sprig of thyme
2 sage leaves
1 bay leaf
150ml / ¹/₄pt / ²/₃ cup olive oil
olive oil, for brushing
1 tsp salt
black pepper
handful of chopped flat-leaf parsley
extra-virgin olive oil, for dressing
crusty bread, to serve

Peel the onion and cut it into eight equal parts. Bang the garlic to loosen the skin. Cut the tomatoes into quarters. Peel the potatoes and pit the olives.

Put all the ingredients except the fish, potatoes, olives and parsley in a heavy pan with pepper to taste. Pour over 300ml / ¹/₂pt water, bring to a boil for 5 minutes,

then add the potatoes. Lower the heat and simmer for 20 minutes, stirring occasionally, until the potatoes are done and start to break up. Remove from the heat, take out the sage and thyme and stir in the olives.

Heat a ridged grill pan until very hot. Brush the fish fillets with olive oil and season with salt and pepper. Grill, skin down, for about 2 minutes.

Stir the parsley into the potato mixture and spoon on to 2 warmed plates. Lay the fillets on top, seared skin side up. Gloss the skin with a few drops of oil and grind some pepper over before serving with crusty bread.

ROAST SANDRE WITH SAFFRON & CORIANDER

Sandre, also known as sander or pike-perch, is a firm white-fleshed freshwater fish, similar – but superior – to perch. If you are unable to obtain sandre, then try cod.

INGREDIENTS FOR 4

2.5 cm / 1in piece of root ginger
2 garlic cloves
1 large hot red chilli, deseeded
3 tbsp sunflower oil, plus more for greasing
$^{1}/_{2}$ tsp red mustard seeds
$^{1}/_{2}$ tsp turmeric
12 strands of saffron, infused in 2 tsp warm water
1 tbsp nam pla Thai fish sauce
4 tbsp white wine vinegar
1 tbsp Thai palm (or light brown) sugar
170g / 6oz / 1 medium tomato, peeled, deseeded
  and diced
150ml / $^{1}/_{4}$pt / $^{2}/_{3}$ cup fish stock
4 sandre or cod fillets, each weighing 200g / 7oz
45g / 1$^{1}/_{2}$oz / 3 tbsp cold unsalted butter, diced
small bunch of coriander
salt and pepper

Preheat the oven to 240°C / 475°F / gas 9.

Peel and chop the ginger and garlic. Remove the

stem and seeds from the chilli and chop finely. Put these 3 ingredients in a processor and whizz to a paste.

Put the sunflower oil in a small heavy saucepan over a low heat. Add the mustard seeds and stir until they start to spit. Take care not to burn them. Stir in the paste from the processor and sweat gently for 2–3 minutes, stirring. Stir in the turmeric and saffron with its liquid. Then add the fish sauce, vinegar and palm sugar. Turn the heat as low as it will go and cook for 3–4 minutes.

Add the diced tomato and fish stock to the sauce, increase the heat to medium and bring to the boil. Lower the heat and simmer for 8 minutes.

Heat a heavy frying pan until very hot. Brush the fish fillets with oil top and bottom, season with salt and pepper and lay them skin side down in the pan. Cook undisturbed for 2–3 minutes, when the skin will have crisped and taken a good dark colour. Transfer to the oven for a final 3 minutes.

As the fish goes into the oven, whisk the butter dice into the sauce. Add the coriander leaves. Immediately spoon the sauce on individual plates and lay the sandre on top, skin side up.

SEA BREAM WITH ROSEMARY BEURRE BLANC

Sea bream is a soft, sweet-tasting fish and perfect for grilling. Served with a beurre blanc scented with rosemary, it makes a very elegant dish.

'Ask your fishmonger to both scale and take the fish off the bone for you, to produce four fillets. Always check yourself for any remaining pin bones, removing them with tweezers.' MW

INGREDIENTS FOR 4

4 sea bream fillets, each weighing about 170g / 6oz
2 tbsp olive oil
extra-virgin olive oil, to dress
salt and pepper

Roast sandre with saffron & coriander

for the sauce beurre blanc:

2 small shallots
1 garlic clove
2 tbsp rosemary leaves
200g / 7oz / 1³/4 sticks unsalted butter
100ml / 3¹/2 fl oz / ¹/2 cup dry white wine
100ml / 3¹/2 fl oz / ¹/2 cup white wine vinegar
3 tbsp double (heavy) cream

Brush the fish fillets with olive oil; season and reserve.

Make the sauce: finely chop the shallots and garlic. Put the rosemary leaves with the shallots and garlic in a pan with 30g / 1oz / 2 tbsp of the butter and sweat gently until soft, but do not colour.

Add the white wine and wine vinegar, increase the temperature and bring to the boil. Reduce quickly until you are left with only 1–2 tablespoons of syrupy residue.

Add the cream and bring to the boil. Lower the heat and whisk in the remaining butter. The sauce will emulsify and become smooth and coherent. Taste and season. Pass through a fine sieve and keep warm.

While finishing the sauce, heat a ridged, dry grill pan until very hot. Lay the fillets on it, skin side down, and cook for 60–90 seconds to char the skin, then turn with a spatula and cook the other side for 2–3 minutes.

During this latter cooking time, spoon 3 tablespoons of sauce on each of 4 warmed plates. Lay the bream on the sauce, skin side up. Brush the skin with a little olive oil to gloss the surface and serve at once.

GRILLED TUNA WITH BEANS & TOMATOES

Tuna is now more widely available, but its quality is often unacceptable. Tuna deteriorates very fast once butchered, which is why the Japanese pay huge premiums for very fresh fish. The flesh should be a shiny moist red and not have an iridescent oily sheen, nor should it be dull-coloured. Both indicate oxidization from exposure to the air.

'Once purchased, keep tuna cling-wrapped and in the fridge until just before you cook it. Eat it the day you buy it. The Quaglino's portion is a generous 200g / 7oz, but you can serve 140g / 5oz ones at home as a little goes a long way.' MW

INGREDIENTS FOR 4

4 tuna steaks cut from the loin, each weighing
  about 140–200g / 5–7oz
5 tbsp extra-virgin olive oil, plus more for brushing
2 lemons, to serve

for the bean and tomato salad:

350g / 12oz fine green beans
extra-virgin olive oil, to dress
4 tomatoes, peeled, deseeded and diced
1 garlic clove, peeled and shaved
4 black olives, pitted
2 tbsp baby capers
12 basil leaves, shredded
handful of picked flat-leaf parsley
salt and pepper

Top and tail the beans and blanch in rapidly boiling salted water until *al dente*, which will take about 3 minutes. Drain and reserve.

Mix the other salad ingredients in a bowl and toss the beans in this while still warm. Mound the bean salad on 4 serving plates.

Heat a dry, ridged grill pan until very hot. Brush the tuna steaks with oil and season with salt and pepper on both sides.

Lay the steaks on the grill at an angle of 45 degrees to the bars. Sear for 30 seconds and turn to sear the other side, laying it in the same direction. Turn after 30 seconds and this time lay at 45 degrees in the opposite direction. Turn finally after 30 seconds, laying it in precisely the same direction. This will produce a neat cross-hatch effect on the surface called quadrillage.

Serve the tuna on top of the beans. Dress with a little extra-virgin oil and put a lemon half on each plate.

YOGHURT-MARINATED BARBECUED LAMB

Yoghurt marinades are common throughout North Africa, The Middle East and India, where they are used to tenderize frankly inferior cuts of meat. Just why yoghurt should have a tenderizing effect is a mystery, but it also works well with the better cuts of meat we enjoy in Britain. It is important to brush the marinade off before cooking as otherwise it tends to cake and burn.

Use a leg of lamb and have your butcher bone it for you, a tricky task and one which you really need to learn how to do if you are to avoid making a hash of it. You also need a boning knife to do the job properly. He will produce a roughly rectangular piece of meat about 5–7.5cm / 2–3in thick, a perfect cut for barbecuing because it will give you some well-done crusty outside bits as well as a succulent pink centre for those who prefer their meat on the rare side.

If you do not want to light a barbecue, then cook on a ridged grill pan.

INGREDIENTS FOR 6

1.8kg / 4lb leg of lamb, boned
juice of 3 limes
1 tsp cumin seeds
1 tsp coriander seeds
1 tsp black peppercorns
2 cloves
2 cm / ³/₄in piece of cinnamon stick
450ml / ³/₄pt / 1²/₃ cups thick natural yoghurt
18 small-to-medium-sized Spanish onions
5 tbsp olive oil
6 garlic cloves
small bunch of fresh thyme
salt and pepper

Two days before you want to cook the lamb: cut the boned leg into 3 pieces, following the seams of skin and fat. Put the pieces into a plastic container in which they will just fit, pour over the lime juice and sprinkle on a little salt. Cling-wrap the top and refrigerate for 24 hours.

The next day: toast the spices in a small, heavy, dry frying pan over a low heat for 2–3 minutes. Grind in a coffee grinder and put into a bowl.

Remove the meat from the container and wipe out any juices from the base. Mix the spices with the yoghurt and spoon this yoghurt marinade on the bottom, lay the lamb on top and cover with the remaining marinade. Rub the marinade well in and return to the fridge for a further 24 hours, removing to return to room temperature at least 2 hours before cooking.

When ready to cook: light the barbecue an hour in advance to obtain maximum heat. Brush off the marinade, sprinkle the meat with salt and lay on the grill, salt side down and about 15cm / 6in above the coals. Do not push it around, but leave it untouched to cook for 8 minutes.

Season the upper surface with salt and pepper before turning and cooking the other side for 7 minutes. Remove and leave to rest in a warm place for 15 minutes before carving across the grain into thick slices.

At the same time as you light the barbecue, preheat the oven to 220°C / 425°F / gas 7 and put on a large, heavy, frying pan to heat over a medium flame.

Peel the onions. Pour the oil into the hot pan, lower the heat and cook the onions, shaking the pan and turning the onions with tongs until they are golden brown all over. Bang the garlic cloves with the heel of your hand and scatter them, unpeeled, around the onions. Scatter the thyme over, and season with salt and pepper. Put into the oven and roast for 30–40 minutes.

Discard the garlic and serve the lamb on warmed plates with 3 onions per person and with the pan juices spooned over.

LOIN OF PORK WITH FENNEL & APPLE

This is an Italian way of roasting pork and uses a boned loin that has been tied into a neat cylinder to give even cooking. Roasting any piece of meat smaller than about 1.8kg / 4lb is never a good idea and this is particularly true of today's pork, which tends to be too lean. We no longer need overcook pork for fear of trichinosis, the parasitic worms caused by swill-feeding. It should be cooked through, but only just. Dry pork is destroyed pork.

'The choice of Granny Smiths is not terribly Italian, but they are the only apples I have found that stay together when roasted in this way.' MW

INGREDIENTS FOR 6–8

2 garlic cloves
2 tsp fennel seeds
3 tbsp olive oil
1.8kg / 4 lb rolled bone loin of pork
4 Granny Smith apples
salt and pepper

Peel the garlic, chop and put in the food processor with the fennel seeds, olive oil and 2 teaspoons of salt. Blitz to a rough purée. Rub the pork all over with this and leave to marinate at room temperature for 3–4 hours.

When ready to cook: preheat the oven to 180°C / 350°F / gas 4. Then roast the pork in a roasting tin for 1¾ hours.

When the meat is done, remove from the tin and rest in a warm place for 20 minutes before carving. Turn up the oven to maximum.

Peel, core and quarter the apples. Put them into the roasting tin, turn with a spoon to coat with the fat and juices and return to the oven for 5–10 minutes.

Carve the pork in 1cm / ½in slices and put on warmed plates with 2–3 pieces of apple on the side and with some of the pan juices spooned over the pork. Serve with crisp roast potatoes or red cabbage.

BRAISED OXTAIL WITH ROOT VEGETABLES & RED WINE

If there is one inexpensive cut of beef which was intended to be elevated to a divine status through slow braising then it is the animal's tail. From such basic beginnings great dishes are created and this one is within the grasp of anybody who is prepared to invest a little time and effort. The French call dishes like this plats mijotés, *that is stews cooked so gently no bubbles burst to the surface of the braising liquid.*

'The current fashion for food preparation being fast is not one for the serious cook who enjoys the unique magic worked by the slowest simmering. It is very important to brown the meat pieces all over before they are stewed. I like the addition of a pig's trotter (foot), as this will give both flavour and body to the sauce.' MW

INGREDIENTS FOR 4

1.2kg / 2½ lb oxtail, cut into pieces
30g / 1oz / 2 tbsp lard or 5 tbsp olive oil
4 shallots
1 garlic clove
1 carrot
2 celery sticks
1 small pig's trotter (foot) [optional]
150g / 5½oz smoked fatty bacon, rind on and
**   in a piece**
3 sprigs of thyme
6 cracked black peppercorns
1 bay leaf
1 bottle of red wine
300ml / ½pt / 1¼ cup chicken stock (see page 138)
salt and pepper
4 tbsp chopped flat-leaf parsley, to garnish
crusty bread, to serve

for the roasting vegetables:
450g / 1lb celeriac

Braised oxtail with root vegetables & red wine

4 large carrots
450g / 1lb pumpkin
4 parsnips
3 tbsp olive oil

Season the oxtail pieces. Heat half the lard or half the oil in a large heavy-bottomed frying pan and, when very hot, brown the meat a few pieces at a time, transferring them to a casserole as they are done. They should be dark brown all over. Don't overcrowd the pan or try to do this too quickly. When all are finished, wipe the pan clean.

Preheat the oven to 140°C / 275°F / gas 1.

Prepare the braising vegetables: peel and trim the shallots, garlic, carrot and celery. Add the remaining lard or oil to the pan and sweat all the braising vegetables gently until dark brown in colour. Add to the oxtail with the trotter, if using bacon, thyme, cracked peppercorns and bay leaf. Pour over the wine and stock. Bring to the boil and skim.

Put on the lid and transfer to the oven for 3 hours, stirring occasionally. Do this gently to avoid breaking up the vegetables.

Towards the end of the cooking time, prepare the roasting vegetables: peel and cut them into 7.5cm / 3in chunks and put into a bowl with the olive oil. Toss to coat. Season with salt and pepper. Heat a pan until shimmering hot and add the vegetables. Brown them on all cut surfaces and transfer to a roasting tin.

The meat is done when it pulls easily off the bone. At this point remove the meat with a slotted spoon, transfer to a warmed plate and reserve.

As you take the casserole from the oven, turn up the temperature to 200°C / 400°F / gas 6 and put the vegetables in to roast. Turn after 15 minutes and baste with the pan juices, then cook for a further 15 minutes, by which time they should be done. If not, give them another 5–10 minutes.

While the vegetables are roasting, strain the braising liquid through a sieve into a pan large enough to hold all the tail pieces and discard everything except the trotter and bacon. Return the liquid to the hob and cook down to a rich glossy sauce. If you have used a trotter it will be almost sticky.

Remove both the trotter and bacon, put the tail pieces and vegetables in the sauce and simmer for 5 minutes to warm through.

Serve on large shallow bowls scattered with lots of chopped parsley; with crusty bread.

ROAST PEPPERED RIB-EYE OF BEEF

Good roast beef begins with the quality of the piece of meat you buy. This should have been aged by the butcher for at least two weeks and perhaps for as long as three. The colour will by then have deepened towards brown, while the meat will have shrunk because of evaporation. Yellowish fat suggests that the animal ate mostly grass, for grain-feeding produces whiter fat. If the meat is bright red then it has not been hung for long enough on the carcass to mature.

Roast beef enthusiasts tend to favour a particular cut and arguably the finest to cook and eat at home is a joint of 5 or 6 wing ribs on the bone. In a Quaglino's context this would be impractical because the meat would be cooked to different degrees on the outside and around the bones. Carving a joint (roast) on the bone is time-consuming and you would inevitably have variations between each serving and unavoidable waste. The restaurant needs to put a precise portion on every plate which has to be cooked medium-rare. Using the flame rotisserie and a carefully boned and tied 3.5kg / 8lb joint (roast) cut from the eye of the middle ribs – a lean cut – this is achieved for every customer. The joint (roast) is wrapped with a thin layer of beef fat by the butcher before it is tied. It is then brushed all over with Dijon mustard and rolled in cracked black pepper.

Because nobody has the kind of flame rotisserie Quag's has, the following method has been tested in a domestic electric oven without convection. It delivers an excellent rare finish, but it is vital to rest the meat for

20 minutes in a warm place before carving across into 2cm / ³/₄in thick slices – just right for a single portion. Serve with a simple gravy made from the pan juices and reduced stock, together with horseradish cream and crisp roast potatoes. If you are serving roast potatoes, allow 170g / 6oz (1–2) per person.

'The importance of resting meats after roasting is absolute and perhaps the least understood part of the cooking process. During resting, the juices which have been forced to the surface are redistributed throughout the meat giving a moist and succulent result. Serving roast meat piping hot is not nearly as important as this. Nevertheless, you should always ensure that your plates and vegetables are very hot when they come to the table. We always make fresh horseradish, which is not always available at retail. However, you can buy good shop-bought horseradish in jars, or alternatively serve with a good Dijon mustard.' MW

INGREDIENTS FOR 8
1.8 kg / 4 lb boned, rolled, barded and tied rib-eye of beef
4 tbsp mignonette peppercorns
1 tbsp sea salt
3 tbsp Dijon mustard
1.35 kg / 3 lb floury (Idaho-type) potatoes
4–6 tbsp beef dripping or olive oil
splash of red wine
300ml / ¹/₂pt / 1¹/₄ cups reduced chicken stock (see page 138)
salt and pepper

for the horseradish cream:
about 2.5cm / 1in piece of fresh horseradish root
300ml / ¹/₂pt / 1¹/₄ cups whipping cream

Remove the meat from the fridge about 2 hours before cooking to bring it to room temperature.

Coarsely crack the peppercorns. You can do this

inside a zip-lock bag with a rolling pin or whizz briefly in a coffee grinder. Mix with the salt and scatter on a Swiss roll tin or shallow tray. Brush the joint (roast) with the mustard, then roll in the pepper and salt. Sit the joint (roast) on a rack in a roasting tin.

Preheat the oven to 220°C / 425°F / gas 7.

Peel the potatoes and cut them into 4cm / 1¹/₂in chunks. Parboil in rapidly boiling salted water for 6 minutes. Drain through a colander and put into a roasting tin with the beef dripping or olive oil, or a mixture of the two. Turn with a spoon to coat evenly. Start them roasting before the beef goes in the oven, turning and basting after 10 minutes. Roast for 15 minutes. Remove from the oven and reserve.

Roast peppered rib-eye of beef

Increase the oven temperature to 240°C / 475°F / gas 9.

When this is reached, put the joint (roast) in the oven for 25 minutes, then lower the temperature to 200°C / 400°F / gas 6 and continue cooking for a further 25 minutes. It is important not to open the oven door for more than a few seconds at any time from start to finish. Remove and rest on its rack for 20 minutes.

Season the potatoes with salt and pepper when you take the beef out and return to the oven. Turn after 10 minutes. They will be done by the time the beef is ready to carve.

While the potatoes are cooking, prepare the horse-radish cream: peel the horseradish. Whip the cream to soft peaks. Grate the horseradish and taste to see how hot it is. Fold however much you like into the cream, tasting until you get the right balance.

While the beef is resting, make a gravy by pouring off the fat from the roasting tin. Put the tin on a high heat and deglaze with a splash of red wine. Add the reduced stock and boil fiercely, scraping and rubbing with the back of a spoon.

Taste and season if needed. Strain. Put a slice of beef in the centre of each warmed plate and spoon on a little gravy. Add some crisp golden-brown potatoes.

Put the horseradish in a bowl on the table for people to help themselves, along with more of the gravy in a sauce-boat.

LAMBS' KIDNEYS WITH BACON & MUSTARD SAUCE

Getting the simplest dishes right is often more difficult than cooking seemingly complex recipes successfully. Here is one such dish, which needs a little extra care in its preparation. Fresh firm kidneys are the first require-ment of this classic treatment. They should be dark and shiny and not smell strongly of uric acid – in making this olfactory judgement, however, don't forget their original ante-mortem function. The older the lamb, the stronger-tasting the kidneys.

'Only ox kidneys need prolonged cooking. Lambs' kidneys should either be cut into small pieces and fried rapidly with very little fat in a pan or cut in halves and grilled. I like them best charcoal-grilled, but you can use a ridged grill pan at home. This needs to be heated from underneath; an overhead grill on a domestic oven is not hot enough. The trick here is to coat them only lightly in oil before putting them on a very hot dry grill. If you have never grilled kidneys this way and are worried by the short cooking time, first try grilling one kidney as instructed. After 3 minutes, cut it open and judge for yourself whether it is done to your liking. In my view they should be oozing a little blood at the centre. If you cook them until well done, they will be tough, resembling rubber.' MW

INGREDIENTS FOR 4
20 small lambs' kidneys
5 tbsp olive oil
12 slices of smoked streaky (thick-cut) bacon
salt and pepper
4 small bunches of watercress, to serve
300 ml / 1/2 pt / 1 1/4 cups Mustard sauce (see page 116)
Mashed potatoes (see page 136), to serve

Remove the fine outer membrane that surrounds the kidneys. Slice each of them in half lengthwise and remove the eyes of fat with either a small, razor-sharp knife or a pair of scissors. Put the oil in a bowl and turn the kidneys in it. Transfer them to a tray and season gen-erously with salt and pepper.

Cut the rinds off the bacon, grill under an overhead grill (broiler) or bake on a rack in a very hot oven until almost cooked. Remove and reserve.

Preheat a dry, ridged grill pan from underneath, until smoking hot. Lay the kidneys on it at an angle of 45 degrees to the ridges, turning them over with tongs after 1 minute and putting them at the same angle to the ridges as before for a further minute.

Turn the kidneys again, this time laying them at 45 degrees to the ridges in the opposite direction for 30 seconds. Turn for the last time, laying in the same direction for a final 30 seconds. This is called quadrillage and gives neat, cross-hatch searing to the meat.

Halfway through the cooking of the kidneys, return the bacon under the grill (broiler) to go crisp.

Serve 10 kidney halves with 3 slices of crisp bacon and a bunch of watercress on each plate.

Pour a little mustard sauce over the kidneys.

Pile the hot mashed potatoes in a bowl with a knob or two of butter on top.

CHICKEN BREASTS WITH CÈPES & SAUTÉ POTATOES

Because the breasts are stuffed with a mixture of parsley, garlic and breadcrumbs this dish is cooked in two stages, with the second using a very hot oven, unlike the classic French sauté which is done entirely on the hob (stove top).

'During the autumn, when fresh cèpes are available, obviously you can use them, but they are horribly expensive. Dried cèpes are good things to have in the store cupboard. A small packet delivers a tremendous amount of flavour and can benefit a wide range of dishes.' MW

INGREDIENTS FOR 4
45g / 1¹/₂oz dried cèpes or porcini
3 large baking potatoes
**4 corn-fed chicken breasts, each weighing about
    170g / 6oz**
100ml / 3¹/₂fl oz / ¹/₂ cup olive oil
**100ml / 3¹/₂fl oz / ¹/₂ cup chicken stock
    (see page 138)**
55g / 2oz / 4 tbsp unsalted butter
1 tbsp chopped parsley
salt and pepper

for the parsley stuffing:
1 garlic clove
3 tbsp chopped parsley
4 tbsp whole breadcrumbs

Put the cèpes or porcini in plenty of cold water to reconstitute for 30–40 minutes. Rinse under running water, rubbing gently to remove residual grit from the stems and pick out any pieces of twig. Press to remove excess liquid and put to dry on paper towels. (Save the strained liquid for a stock.)

Parboil the potatoes in their skins for 15–20 minutes, or until just cooked. Peel when cool enough to handle and cut across into 5mm / ¹/₄in slices. Reserve.

Prepare the stuffing: peel and chop the garlic. Put into the food processor with the parsley, breadcrumbs and a little salt and pepper and whizz to mix evenly. Working from one side, carefully pull the skin away from each chicken breast leaving it attached at both ends and along the other side. Spoon a quarter of the stuffing into each pocket. Brush the breasts on both sides with a little of the olive oil, season lightly with salt and pepper and reserve.

Preheat the oven to 240°C / 475°F / gas 9 and put a heavy skillet over a low-to-medium heat.

Lay the chicken in the pan, skin and stuffing upwards and cook for 5 minutes. Transfer to a roasting tin in which it will fit snugly, pour round the chicken stock and put in the oven to finish cooking, which will take between 6 and 8 minutes. Remove and transfer to a warmed plate. Cover and keep warm.

At the same time as you start to cook the chicken, pour half the remaining olive oil in a large frying pan into which the sliced potatoes will fit in 1 layer (or use 2 pans). Slowly sauté the potatoes over a medium heat. Brown the bottom surface before turning.

In a second pan, sauté the cèpes or porcini gently in the remaining oil. When the potatoes are golden brown and nicely crisped on both sides, stir in the cèpes or porcini, the butter and the parsley. Turn off the heat and keep warm.

Spoon the potato and mushroom mixture on warmed serving plates. Cut each breast into 2 and at an angle and place on top. Spoon any remaining parsley butter over the chicken.

ROAST GUINEA FOWL WITH BLACK OLIVE BUTTER SAUCE

Guinea fowl are really farmed game, sharing qualities of chicken, squab and pheasant. They have a pronounced and delicious flavour, but are not remotely high-tasting and, being virtually fat-free, need sensitive and finely timed cooking if they are not to be too dry. The best way to achieve a perfect result is to seal the bird before it goes into the oven, a restaurant technique used to save time that can be used in the domestic kitchen to good effect. They do not take a lot of roasting and 30 minutes in an oven preheated to 240°C / 475°F / gas 9 will be enough for a 1.1kg / 2¹/₂lb bird.

'A 10-minute rest after coming out of the oven and before carving will ensure an even distribution of juices in the meat, giving a uniformly tender and moist result. One guinea fowl will serve two people generously.' MW

INGREDIENTS FOR 2

450g / 1lb new potatoes
2 garlic cloves
1 tbsp rosemary leaves
55g / 2oz / 4 tbsp softened butter
3 tbsp olive oil
1 dressed guinea fowl, weighing about 1.1kg / 2¹/₂lb
salt and pepper

for the black olive butter sauce:
115g / 4oz / 1 stick unsalted butter
1 small garlic clove, peeled, smashed and finely chopped
75g / 2¹/₂oz / ²/₃ cup stoned black olives, chopped

12 juniper berries
2 shallots, finely chopped
30g / 1oz / 2 tbsp butter
100ml / 3¹/₂fl oz / ¹/₂ cup brandy
150ml / ¹/₄pt / ²/₃ cup Madeira
200ml / 7 fl oz / ³/₄ cup chicken stock (see page 138)
150ml / ¹/₄pt / ²/₃ cup double (heavy) cream

First start the black olive butter sauce: cream the butter until white then add the garlic and the stoned olives. Mix evenly and roll into a tube in cling film. Refrigerate. This can be done the day before or you can make a larger amount and freeze it (it will keep very well.

Boil the potatoes in salted water for 15–20 minutes, or until just cooked. Refresh them in cold water, then drain and reserve.

Preheat the oven to 240°C / 475°F / gas 9.

Peel, smash and chop the 2 garlic cloves and work in 1 teaspoon each of salt and ground black pepper. Take the rosemary leaves, chop them and mix half of them with half of the softened butter along with the garlic, salt and pepper paste.

Heat a dry heavy frying pan until very hot. Add the olive oil and, as it starts to smoke, lay the bird in it, one breast downwards, and seal. Turn and repeat on the other breast, then on the legs and back until all the surfaces are golden brown.

Season liberally with salt and pepper, push most of the rosemary butter into the cavity and smear the rest over the breast and legs. Transfer to a rack over a roasting tray, breast upwards, and roast for 20–25 minutes.

While the bird is roasting, finish the sauce: first sweat the juniper berries and finely chopped shallots in all but a knob of the remaining butter. Turn up the heat and add the brandy and Madeira. Swirl and ignite to flame, shaking the pan. Then add the chicken stock and reduce by half.

Pass through a fine sieve into a clean pan. Add the cream, bring to the boil and finish by whisking in pieces of the chilled olive butter.

Roast guinea fowl with black olive butter sauce

Also while the bird is roasting, cut the potatoes in half lengthwise and sauté them in olive oil, adding the remaining rosemary leaves and the coarsely chopped garlic after 10 minutes. Add the reserved knob of butter and season with salt and pepper before serving.

Remove the bird from the oven and rest for 10 minutes, before carving off the legs, thighs and breasts. Serve with the potatoes and with the sauce poured over and round the meat.

BOUDIN BLANC WITH MUSTARD SAUCE & MASH

One item that sits as happily in a grand restaurant as in a café or brasserie is boudin blanc, the delicate creamy sausage of chicken mousse and pork that you can dress up or down as fancy and ambience dictate. It is expensive to buy and time-consuming rather than difficult to make. For some reason the idea of home-made sausages still strikes people as rather adventurous. Natural hog casings can be bought from your butcher, dried and salted in tins. All you have to do is rinse them and soak overnight in cold water.

'If you do not have a mixer with a sausage-making attachment then buy a hand-operated sausage pump. They are similar to icing kits, but on a slightly larger scale. If all else fails, use a piping bag and plain nozzle to fill the casings.' MW

INGREDIENTS FOR 6

4–5 shallots
1 garlic clove
55g / 2oz / 4 tbsp butter, plus more for coating
450g / 1lb chicken breasts
225g / 8oz lean pork loin
170g / 6oz white pork-back fat
whites of 2 eggs
300ml / ¹/₂pt / 1¹/₄ cups double (heavy) cream
1 tbsp chopped parsley

1 tbsp chopped sage
¹/₂ nutmeg, grated
1 or 2 lengths of salted hog casings
salt and white pepper
Mashed potatoes (see page 136), to serve
milk, for poaching

for the mustard sauce:
2 shallots
25g / ³/₄oz / 1¹/₂ tbsp unsalted butter
2 tbsp white wine
100ml / 3¹/₂fl oz / ¹/₂ cup chicken stock (see page 138)
450ml / ³/₄pt / 1²/₃ cup double (heavy) cream
4 tbsp Dijon mustard
pepper

Make the boudin several days ahead: first soak an appropriate length of the hog casing in water overnight.

Next day: rinse the hog casings, drain and reserve. Peel the shallots and garlic and finely chop. Sweat them in butter for 2–3 minutes, until just softened. Reserve.

Skin the chicken breasts and cut into 2.5cm / 1in cubes. Cube the pork in the same way and cut the back fat off the rind (keeping the rind for another dish, like cassoulet) and cube. Put them all together in a food processor and blitz to a purée. Push this through a sieve into a bowl sitting on ice cubes inside a larger bowl.

Beat the egg whites gradually into the forcemeat. Add the cream, continuing to beat with a wooden or plastic spatula until you have a silky homogenous mass. Work in the parsley, shallots and sage. Season with nutmeg, salt and pepper and stir in thoroughly. Test for seasoning by poaching a spoonful in simmering water. Taste and adjust accordingly.

Fill the hog casings, but do not overfill or they will burst. Twist and knot with thin string at 13–15cm / 5–6in intervals. Prick each one with a pin 4 or 5 times and put them in a wide shallow pan. Pour equal quantities of milk and water to cover and bring them to just below boiling point. Poach them for 18 minutes. The ideal temperature is 90°C / 195°F, hot enough to cook them in this time, but not so hot that they burst. A thermometer is the best way of ensuring this. They should also stay immersed throughout the cooking time and the easiest way of doing this is to cover them with a cloth.

Leave to cool completely in the cooking liquid. Then transfer to a plastic-lidded box and refrigerate the boudins for several days. Like all sausages, they benefit from a maturation period.

On the day of serving, first make the sauce: peel and dice the shallots. Sweat them in the butter until soft but without colour. Add the white wine and stock and reduce at a rapid boil by two-thirds. Add the cream and reduce by one third, then add the mustard. Season with pepper, pass through a sieve and reserve.

Carefully make a shallow incision down one side of each boudin and peel off the skins. Roll them in melted butter and grill (broil) or pan-fry gently for 4 minutes, turning once after 2 minutes, when they will be striped golden-brown top and bottom.

Serve very hot with buttery Mashed potatoes and the mustard sauce.

ROAST DUCK WITH BOK-CHOY

The Chinese are the masters of duck roasting. While they do all sorts of things which are beyond all but the specialists, like inflating the skin away from the flesh prior to cooking, we can emulate some of their techniques to achieve a beautifully glossy and crisp-skinned finish.

'The secret of our method is maltose (malt sugar), not very Cantonese but certainly effective. Bok-choy is a dark-leafed brassica with crisp white stems. It is now grown in this country and available in supermarkets.' MW

INGREDIENTS FOR 4

1 dressed duck, weighing about 2.25kg / 5lb
4 tbsp malt vinegar
55g / 2oz maltose (malt sugar)
1 tbsp ginger juice
1 tbsp rice flour
2 heads of bok-choy

for the sauce:
5cm / 2in piece of root ginger
6 spring onions (scallions)
small bunch of coriander, roots on
3 tbsp dark sesame oil
4 pieces of star anise
1 tbsp Szechuan pepper
1 litre / 1³/₄pt / 4¹/₃ cups chicken stock
   (see page 38)
100ml / 3 ¹/₂fl oz / ¹/₂ cup Kikkoman soy sauce
4 tbsp cornflour (cornstarch)

Bring a big pan of water to the boil. Put a butcher's hook through the neck end of the duck. Add the vinegar to the water, then plunge the duck into it and blanch for 60 seconds. Remove and hang up to dry in a cool airy place, preferably overnight.

When the duck is almost dry, warm the maltose over a pan of simmering water. Add the ginger juice then stir in the rice flour to thicken to a fairly liquid paste.

As soon as the paste is cool enough to touch, use your hands to give the duck a massage with it, as if you were rubbing in tanning lotion. Watch out: if too hot, maltose will give you a nasty burn. Leave to stand for 30 minutes before cooking.

Preheat the oven to 180°C / 350°F / gas 4. Put the duck on a rack over a tin with 2.5cm / 1in of water in the base and roast for 50–60 minutes, when you will have a dark brown and crisp skin, concealing slightly pink moist flesh. Remove and leave to rest for 20 minutes on the rack.

While the duck is resting, make the sauce: peel the ginger, top and tail the spring onions and wash the

coriander including the roots, then chop all finely.

Put a pan on a medium heat and, when hot, add the sesame oil followed by the star anise and Szechuan pepper and fry them, stirring until they release their aroma and start to colour.

Add the chopped vegetables and sweat for 2–3 minutes, then pour on the chicken stock and soy sauce. Increase the heat and bring to the boil. Lower the heat and simmer until reduced by half.

Mix the cornflour to a paste with cold water and stir into this sauce to thicken it. Lower the heat and simmer for 5 minutes, then pass through a sieve into a clean pan. Taste, adding a little more soy sauce if needed and keep warm.

Trim the base of the bok-choy, separate the leaves and blanch them in rapidly boiling salted water for between 1 and 2 minutes.

Carve the duck by removing the legs and thighs and the whole breasts. Cut the breasts into 2, placing a half on each of 4 warmed serving plates accompanied by a leg or a thigh.

Put some drained bok-choy next to the duck and pour a little of the sauce around and on top of the duck before serving.

SQUAB WITH BROAD BEANS, OLIVES & SAGE LEAVES

The price of grain-fed squab pigeon is still far too high, as the majority of birds are imported from France. The Italians are now producing them as well but, at the time of writing, no British squab are commercially raised – a lack of initiative for which there seems to be no logical rationale.

If you can't get the giblets with the squab then use a strong chicken stock reduction (see page 138) for the sauce. The broad beans we use are fresh from the pod, but these are not always obtainable. Frozen small beans can then be substituted. The potatoes are late-season, having formed a skin.

Squab with broad beans, olives & sage leaves

INGREDIENTS FOR 4

675g / 1¹/₂lb new potatoes
2 tbsp chopped flat-leaf parsley
150ml / ¹/₄pt / ²/₃ cup extra-virgin olive oil
12 sage leaves
4 garlic cloves
4 squab pigeons
3 tbsp olive oil
sunflower oil, for deep-frying
225g / 8oz broad beans (fava beans)
salt and pepper

for the pigeon jus:
115g / 4oz pigeon wings, necks and giblets,
   including liver
2 tbsp olive oil
1 carrot
12 mushroom stalks
4 shallots
1 celery stick
1 garlic clove
5 tbsp Madeira
575ml / 1pt / 2¹/₂ cups chicken stock
   (see page 138)
2 sage leaves

Make the jus: fry the pigeon wings, necks and the giblets (not the liver) in a little oil until browned. Chop the carrot, mushroom stalks, shallots and celery and add to the pan with the whole garlic clove. Sauté briefly, deglaze with the Madeira and cook down to a syrupy residue. Add the stock and reduce by half. Chop the livers, add and cook briefly. Pass through a fine sieve into a clean pan. Add the sage leaves and reserve.

Preheat the oven to 200°C / 400°F / gas 6 and put a roasting tin for the squab in the oven.

Peel the new potatoes and boil until soft. Drain, mash roughly with a fork in a bowl, add the parsley and season adding the olive oil. Keep warm.

Heat a heavy frying pan. Put a sage leaf and a peeled garlic clove in each bird. Brush the outside with olive

MAIN COURSES

oil and season generously with salt and pepper. Then brown all over in the pan. Transfer to the hot roasting tin, baste with olive oil and roast for 8–10 minutes. Remove and rest in a warm place for 5 minutes.

As the squab go into the oven, preheat sunflower oil in a deep-fryer or in a pan to 190°C / 375°F and boil a pan of salted water for the beans. Blanch for 2 minutes, drain, and shell.

Boil the sauce and keep warm. Fry the remaining sage leaves in 2 batches for 5–6 seconds to crisp. Beware, they will spit! Remove and drain on paper towels. Carve the breasts and legs from the birds.

Put a big scoop of potato on the centre of each plate and arrange the breasts and legs on top. Spoon beans around the potatoes and drizzle these with a little olive oil. Pour a little jus over the pigeon and garnish with the crisp sage leaves.

CONFIT OF DUCK WITH ROCKET/ARUGULA

Confit – salted meat, poached and preserved in its own fat – stems from the south-west of France. The technique is most notably associated with goose and duck, though it is also used to cook and store pork. Indeed, lard is an important part of the process, particularly if you do not have large amounts of goose or duck fat to work with, as it can substitute for either or can be added to small amounts of duck or goose fat.

Quaglino's uses only duck legs for confit, but getting hold of them in retail outlets will be problematic. Instead, buy leg-and-thigh portions from the supermarket, cutting them into two through the joint. You cannot have confit without fat; but you can salt more lightly, cook more gently and serve with sharp clean-tasting rocket (arugula) leaves rather than the traditional accompaniment of shallow-fried potatoes.

The crispness of the duck skin in this dish is one of the most delicious aspects of the confit, the result of the two-stage cooking which extracts the subcutaneous fat.

'A little confit is a magical addition to other dishes like cassoulet or garbure, while the fat is brilliant for roasting potatoes or basting a turkey. It can be strained and used at least three times for making confit, before the salt build-up makes it unpalatable. Make the confit at least a week before you eat it to allow the flavour to develop fully.' MW

INGREDIENTS FOR 4
4 duck leg-and-thigh joints
55g / 2oz / 1/3 cup Maldon sea salt
4 sprigs of thyme
2 bay leaves
1 tsp black pepper
1.3kg / 3lb duck fat
large bunch of rocket (arugula) leaves
4 tbsp balsamic vinegar

At least a week before serving: first cut through the duck portions at the joint to separate legs from thighs. Scatter a layer of salt into a metal tray. Break up the thyme, crumble the bay leaves, and rub them into the duck with the pepper. Lay the duck portions on the salt. Scatter the remaining salt and herbs on top and refrigerate overnight.

Next day, remove the duck portions from the tray and brush the salt off each with a damp cloth. Do not leave them for more than 24 hours or the confit will be too salty.

Melt the fat in a large pan. Immerse the legs, bring to the boil, and immediately lower the heat and gently simmer for approximately 2 1/2 hours. Push a skewer in to test to see if it is done. If not absolutely tender, continue cooking for another 20–30 minutes. Remove from the heat and, when cool, transfer the duck pieces to a plate and refrigerate.

Put the fat into a bowl and refrigerate until set hard. Remove, upend the fat into a tin, and take off the rich meat jelly which will have set at the base. This jelly makes a delicious addition to any gravy or meat sauce (if you leave it with the fat it will, in time, go bad and ruin the whole confit). Bring the fat back to the boil, then remove from the heat.

When cool, ladle a layer into the bottom of the container in which you are going to store the confit. Plastic boxes with lids are ideal. Leave to set, then lay the duck pieces on top and ladle over fat to cover.

The day of serving: preheat the oven to 180°C / 350°F / gas 4. Remove the pieces of duck from the fat and scrape off as much fat as you can. Place the pieces skin side down in a frying pan over a low heat and when they start to fry, put into the oven for 10 minutes, when the skin will be crisp and brown.

Wash and dry the rocket. Place in a bowl and dress with the balsamic vinegar. Mound the leaves on individual plates with confit in the centre and serve while the duck is hot.

ROAST POUSSIN WITH POLENTA & CAULIFLOWER

A juicy roast poussin for each person is served with creamy polenta studded with buttery cauliflower. Putting them together in this way enhances all the ingredients, a definite case of the sum of the parts being greater than any of its components.

'One evening in the kitchen at the home of John Torode, then my sous chef and now chef at Mezzo, we decided we would try every combination we could think of to come up with the perfect formula for instant polenta. This was our sixth attempt, but worth the effort. The thing which really made all the difference was the inclusion of Mascarpone.' MW

INGREDIENTS FOR 4

1 cauliflower, weighing about 450g / 1lb
55g / 2oz / 4tbsp unsalted butter, plus more for greasing
4 poussins, each weighing about 300g / 10½oz

for the stuffing:
1 garlic clove
8 sage leaves
4 tbsp olive oil
½ tsp salt
¼ tsp ground black pepper

for the polenta:
2 garlic cloves
300ml / ½pt / 1¼ cups full-fat milk
100g / 3½oz / ⅔ cup Valsugana 'instant' polenta
125ml / 4fl oz / ½ cup double (heavy) cream
45g / 1½oz / ½ cup grated Parmesan
75g / 2½oz Mascarpone

Preheat the oven to 220°C / 425°F / gas 7 and butter an ovenproof dish.

Trim the base off the cauliflower and break the head into florets. Melt the butter in a saucepan, add the florets, season lightly with salt and pepper and sweat gently for 12–15 minutes until translucent. Remove from the heat, put in a bowl and reserve.

Make the polenta: peel, smash and chop the garlic and put into a saucepan with 200ml / 7fl oz / ⅞ cup of water, the milk and some salt and pepper. Bring to a rolling boil, add the polenta and stir until it thickens to a smooth porridge (about 4 minutes). Turn down the heat and add the cream and all but 2 tablespoons of the Parmesan. Continue to stir until fully amalgamated. Remove from the heat and stir in the Mascarpone.

Pour the polenta over the cauliflower, mix with a spoon then pour into the prepared ovenproof dish.

Make the stuffing: peel the garlic and chop finely. Finely chop the sage and mix together. Fill the cavities

of the birds with this mixture and brush them all over liberally with olive oil. Season with pepper.

Put 3 tablespoons of oil in a large heavy frying pan to heat until smoking hot. Lay the birds in, breast down and brown them, turning until they have a good golden colour all over. Then transfer to the roasting tin in the oven, breasts upwards. Sprinkle on a generous amount of sea salt and put to roast.

Baste after 5 minutes and put the polenta in the bottom of the oven. After another 5 minutes, baste the poussins again. Continue cooking for another 5 minutes, when the birds will have had 15 minutes and the polenta 10. Push a skewer into the thickest point of a poussin leg to check whether they are done. If pink juices run, give them another 3–5 minutes. Remove, transfer to a warm place and rest for 5–10 minutes.

When you take the birds out of the oven, sprinkle the polenta with the reserved grated Parmesan and move it up to the middle of the oven. Reduce the temperature setting to 200°C / 400°F / gas 6.

After 10 minutes, both the poussins and the polenta will be ready to serve.

RABBIT WITH PROSCIUTTO & HERBS

Rabbit is a virtually fat-free meat, so it needs to be sensitively treated and cooked if it is not to be dry. Here this is achieved by stuffing the boned legs with butter before wrapping them in sheets of prosciutto. The restaurant serves this dish with roast pumpkin, though you could serve any roast root vegetables or potatoes.

'For a chef there is a huge difference between working in London and Western Australia, and that is in the availability of ingredients and being able to specify precisely to your suppliers what you want. In this case we are able to buy only the back legs with the femur bones removed and with no holes in the skin. You may not be so fortunate with your butcher. If you have to buy whole rabbits then use the saddles and front legs in another dish, such as a casserole with peppers and thyme.' MW

INGREDIENTS FOR 4

170g / 6oz / 1^1/$_2$ sticks unsalted butter
15g / ^{1}/$_2$oz / 1 cup chopped fresh tarragon
15g / ^{1}/$_2$oz / 1 cup parsley
8g / ^{1}/$_4$oz / ^{1}/$_2$ cup sage leaves
^{1}/$_4$ tsp salt
^{1}/$_4$ tsp pepper
4 large boned rabbit legs
4 large slices of prosciutto (Parma ham)
675g / 1^1/$_2$lb pumpkin
4 tbsp olive oil
4 bunches of watercress, to serve

Using an electric whisk, beat the butter in a bowl until white. Chop the herbs and whisk into the butter with the salt and pepper.

Open out each leg and spoon a quarter of the mixture down the middle. Fold the flesh over and tuck the skin in like an envelope. Wrap a slice of prosciutto around each leg tightly to give a neat inverted cone and refrigerate for 30 minutes to firm. Alternatively, this can be done the day before.

Preheat the oven to 200°C / 400°F / gas 6.

Cut off the rind from the pumpkin, remove the seeds and cut the flesh into 7.5cm / 3in chunks. Toss in a bowl with the olive oil to coat. Season with salt and pepper and brown the cut surfaces in a hot pan. Transfer to a roasting tin and place in the oven. After 15 minutes, turn the pieces.

Roast the legs in a roasting tin for 15–20 minutes. Remove and rest for 5–8 minutes. Cut into 2, and serve adding any pan juices and the pumpkin, which should be done by this point. Garnish with watercress.

Rabbit with prosciutto & herbs

ROAST PHEASANT WITH GIROLLES & TOMATO TARRAGON SAUCE

Pheasant, once an expensive bird eaten by the privileged few, is now remarkably cheap, as more and more birds are specially reared and released to be shot immediately. They still have to be plucked and you can either ask your butcher or game dealer to do this for you or have a go yourself. It is not difficult, merely time-consuming. You will then have to draw the insides out of the bird, not a job for the faint-hearted.

Somewhat confusingly, girolles is the French term for the wild mushroom that in this country goes by the name chanterelles – another French word. Figure that one out!

'Pheasants need to be hung before they become tender and flavourful, but how long you hang them will depend on the temperature and humidity. The only way to be sure of how long they have been hung is to shoot them yourself or go to a good game dealer. If you can't get hold of girolles, use any other wild mushroom or, at a pinch, more field mushrooms.' MW

INGREDIENTS FOR 4
2 pheasants
55g / 2oz / 4 tbsp unsalted butter, softened

for the sauce:
6 banana shallots (see page 66)
2 garlic cloves
140g / 5oz / 1³/₄ cups field mushrooms
55g / 2oz / 4 tbsp unsalted butter
4 plum tomatoes, peeled, deseeded and diced
2 tbsp chopped tarragon
300ml / ¹/₂pt / 1¹/₄ cups white wine
500ml / 17fl oz / 2 cups chicken stock (see page 138)
170g / 6oz / 2 cups girolles
salt and pepper

Preheat the oven to 220°C / 425°F / gas 7.

Smear the pheasants inside and out with the softened butter and season generously with salt and pepper. Place them breast down in a tin and roast for 20 minutes. Baste with the pan juices and return to the oven, breast up. Baste again after 10 minutes. Remove from the oven 10 minutes later, when they have had a total of 40 minutes. Leave to rest in a warm place for 10–15 minutes.

Make the sauce when the pheasants go in the oven (or it can mostly be made earlier and finished just before serving): peel and finely chop half the shallots and the garlic. Trim the base off the field mushroom stalks and chop. Sweat the shallots, garlic and chopped mushrooms in half the butter until softened.

Add the tomatoes to the pan with one-quarter of the tarragon. Stir, increase the heat to medium and cook for 5 minutes. Add the wine and reduce at a rapid boil until nearly dry. Add the stock and reduce again by half. Taste, season with salt and pepper, pass through a sieve and reserve. The sauce can be made up to this point and held.

To finish the sauce: slice the remaining shallots across into thin rings. Sweat in the remaining butter until soft, then add the girolles and sauté briefly. Stir into the sauce, adding the remaining tarragon.

Carve the pheasants by removing the legs and thighs and the whole breasts. Serve a leg, a thigh and a breast each. Spoon the sauce and mushrooms around. This is excellent with mashed potatoes, or creamed parsnips.

SPICY POTATO CAKES WITH CHICKPEAS & CORIANDER

'This may seem a little surreal in the Quag's context, but is hugely popular and is one of our most frequently requested vegetarian dishes. Any potatoes will do, but large floury (Idaho-type) baking potatoes are best. You can buy garam masala – fragrant spice mixes – or make your own. There is no definitive recipe, but the one given below is very good.' MW

INGREDIENTS FOR 4

200g / 7oz / 7/8 cup chickpeas
675g / 1 1/2lb baking potatoes
2 red chillies, deseeded and finely chopped
large handful of coriander leaves
flour, for dusting
6 tomatoes
125ml / 4fl oz / 1/2 cup sunflower oil
1 tsp dark mustard seeds
1 tsp chilli powder
salt and pepper

for the garam masala:
2cm / 3/4in piece of cinnamon stick
2 whole cloves
1 tsp cumin seeds
1 tsp black peppercorns
1/2 tsp cardamom seeds
1/2 tsp nutmeg

The day before: make the garam masala. Whizz the ingredients together in a coffee grinder to a fine powder and store in a screw-top jar.

Soak the chickpeas in water overnight.

Next day: drain the chickpeas, put into a pan and cover with cold water by about 2.5cm / 1in. Bring to the boil, lower to a simmer and cook for about 1 1/2–3 hours or until tender. Salt towards the end of cooking. Leave to cool in their cooking liquid.

Steam or boil the unpeeled potatoes for 20 minutes, or until they give in the centre when you push in a skewer. Drain and, as soon as they are cool enough to handle, peel and grate coarsely into a bowl.

Transfer about one-third to another bowl and to this add the chillies and 2 tablespoons of the coriander. Add 1 teaspoon of the garam masala (keep the rest for making curries, it stores well), salt and pepper, and mix well with a fork. Divide into 4 and roll into balls.

Divide the remaining two-thirds of the potato into 4 and shape into flattened rounds, making a depression in the middle of each. Put the spiced balls on top and pull the potato up and around to form an outer layer. Push down and shape into cakes about 4cm / 1 1/2in thick. Put on a lightly floured tray and cover with a cloth.

Blanch the tomatoes in boiling water for 10–15 seconds, refresh in cold water and peel. Cut into fine dice (concassé) and reserve.

In a saucepan, put 3 tablespoons of the sunflower oil and, when hot, add the mustard seeds and stir. Sizzle for 10 seconds, then stir in the chilli powder. Have a handkerchief ready, as the pungent vapours given off will make you cough and your eyes run. Add the tomato concassé and fry for 2 minutes, stirring.

Then put in the chickpeas with their cooking liquid and bring to the boil. Lower the heat and simmer gently for 30 minutes. At this point taste, adding more salt and pepper if needed.

Put the remaining sunflower oil in a frying pan large enough to hold the cakes – not touching each other – or use 2 pans. Fry gently over a medium heat. Do not touch them for at least 5 minutes so the bottom surface can crisp and brown. Turn and fry the other sides.

Add the remaining coriander leaves to the chickpeas and stir in. Spoon on to 4 deep serving plates and sit a potato cake on top.

Spaghetti with rocket (arugula) & roasted tomatoes

SPAGHETTI WITH ROCKET/ ARUGULA & ROASTED TOMATOES

Rocket is one of the most fashionable leaves around. Also called rucola and arugula – even roquette – it is an intense green colour and has a lovely peppery flavour. People tend to think of it as a salad ingredient, but it is also excellent cooked in soups or, as here, wilted by the heat of the spaghetti.

'At Quaglino's we use fresh spaghetti, not least for speed of service and consistent delivery; but a good-quality dried pasta is ideal, for a perfect al dente finish.' MW

INGREDIENTS FOR 4
4 tbsp pesto
2 tbsp extra-virgin olive oil, plus more for serving
115g / 4oz Pecorino
4 handfuls of rocket (arugula) leaves
4 tbsp balsamic vinegar
12 Roast tomato halves (see page 137)
350g / 12oz best-quality dried spaghetti
salt and pepper

Thin the pesto with the olive oil and reserve. Shave 8 slices from the block of cheese. Crumble the remaining cheese into small pieces. Dress the rocket with the balsamic vinegar and reserve. At this point you should have the tomato halves ready.

Cook the spaghetti in masses of rapidly boiling salted water for 8–10 minutes until *al dente*. Drain through a colander and transfer to a large bowl while there are still drops of water adhering to the strands.

Toss the spaghetti with two-thirds of the pesto oil to give a uniform thin coating, then add the rocket and crumbled cheese. Toss again gently. Season to taste.

Put 3 tomato halves on each of 4 warmed plates and mound the spaghetti mixture on top. Top each with shavings of cheese and dribble over a little more oil. Finish with more ground pepper.

POLENTA WITH GORGONZOLA & WILD MUSHROOMS

Polenta, once the food of the poorest peasants in northern Italy, is now fashionable fare. It can be very basic, like tasteless yellow gruel, or it can be dressed up to make a fabulous main course. Vegetarian customers at Quag's complain bitterly in the brief periods when it is left off the menu. Polenta has its traditionalists who insist it can only be made from coarsely ground cornmeal in a copper pot and stirred with a wooden spoon over a wood fire for 45 minutes.

'While we do use unmodified polenta in the restaurant, food technologists have given the world instant polenta which, treated sympathetically, gives an excellent result. Enriched with cream and Gorgonzola, scented with wild mushrooms and garlic, polenta can be extraordinary.' MW

INGREDIENTS FOR 6
55g / 2oz / 4 tbsp butter
200g / 7oz Gorgonzola
85g / 3oz Reggiano Parmesan
375g / 13oz / $3^7/_8$ cups polenta (Star or Valsugana 'instant' variety)
2 tsp salt
1 tsp ground black pepper
300ml / $^1/_2$pt / $1^1/_4$ cups double (heavy) cream
115g / 4oz / $1^1/_2$ cups wild mushrooms

Preheat the oven to 150°C / 300°F / gas 2 and butter an ovenproof dish.

Cut two-thirds of the Gorgonzola into 5cm / 2in chunks and grate the Parmesan. Reserve.

Bring 1.5 litre / $2^1/_2$pts / $6^1/_4$ cups of water to a fast boil and pour in the polenta, stirring until smooth. Season with the salt and pepper and cook for 5 minutes, stirring. Bubbles rise to the surface and burst like volcanic lava. It can spatter and burn you, so beware.

Add the cream slowly, continuing to stir, then the Parmesan. Remove from the heat and cool for 5 minutes, stirring intermittently.

Next, stir in the Gorgonzola chunks, but do not mix too thoroughly. Pour into the buttered ovenproof dish (you want a depth of about 7.5cm / 3in). Smooth the top flat. Cover the top completely with shavings of the reserved Gorgonzola.

Bake the polenta for 40 minutes. Cut into 6 squares and serve immediately or leave to cool, then cut and reheat wrapped in foil.

Just before bringing to the table, wipe the mushrooms, discarding any woody stalks and sauté in the remaining butter. Put a large spoonful on each plate next to the polenta.

LASAGNE WITH WILD MUSHROOMS & TRUFFLE OIL

Lasagne is still most often eaten in its classic Bolognese version, with layers of rich meat ragù and béchamel. This version uses wild mushrooms and is served seasonally with truffle shaved over. If you are a mushroom hunter, then any mixture of woodland fungi will do. If you wish to buy fresh cèpes then grit your teeth – there is no getting away from the expense of these ingredients. However, help is to hand: by adding a small percentage of dried cèpes to flat-cap cultivated mushrooms and spiking the mixture with a little truffle oil you will have a delicious lasagne without breaking the bank. You can buy Italian porcini in small packets.

Substitution is never acceptable in a restaurant context, where the customer pays for precisely what it says a dish contains on the menu. However, a sympathetic variation on a theme is the point where the private cook shakes hands with the real world.

Quag's always uses sheets of fresh pasta for lasagne, but the pre-cooked dried lasagne that requires no preliminary boiling is very good, though it needs rather more liquid in the sauces.

INGREDIENTS FOR 6

55g / 2oz / 4 tbsp butter
55g / 2oz / $^1/_2$ cup flour
900ml / 1$^1/_2$pt / 3$^3/_4$ cups milk
$^1/_4$ nutmeg, grated
150ml / $^1/_4$pt / $^2/_3$ cup double (heavy) cream
450g / 1lb flat-cap cultivated mushrooms
30g / 1oz / 2 cups dried cèpes
3 garlic cloves
large handful of flat-leaf parsley
4 tbsp olive oil
225g / 8oz packet pre-cooked lasagne
1 tbsp truffle oil, plus more for serving (optional)
salt and pepper
85g / 3oz / 1 cup fresh Parmesan, to serve
1 small white truffle (optional), to serve

Soak dried cèpes in 150ml / $^1/_4$pt hot water for 20 minutes. Rinse and serve.

Make a roux with the butter and flour, and cook gently for 2 minutes before adding the milk and bringing slowly to the boil, while whisking all the time.

Lower the temperature to a simmer.

Season with salt, pepper and grated nutmeg and cook for at least 20 minutes over the lowest heat possible, stirring occasionally with a wooden spoon and pushing right to the edge of the pan. If you don't do so the béchamel will stick and burn. The consistency should be that of single (light) cream. Remove the sauce from the heat, stir in the cream and reserve.

While the béchamel is cooking, wipe the mushrooms and remove the stems. Cut the caps into 1cm / $^1/_2$in slices.

Peel and chop the garlic and finely chop the parsley.

Sauté the mushrooms and reconstituted cèpes in the olive oil. When they wilt and exude water, add the garlic, tossing and stirring. Cook for a further 2 minutes. Stir in the parsley, remove from the heat and season.

Preheat the oven to 200°C / 400°F / gas 6 and brush the sides and base of a 25 x 20cm / 10 x 8in rectangular ovenproof dish with olive oil.

Spoon enough béchamel on the base of the dish to cover, then lay 4 sheets of pasta on top. Mix together the mushrooms with the remaining béchamel. Spoon a layer of this over the pasta.

Repeat with another 4 sheets of the pasta on top. Add another layer of mushroom sauce, and end with a final layer of pasta sheets.

It can now be left to stand for an hour or so before cooking or can be refrigerated overnight; if so, remove from the fridge and allow to return to room temperature before baking.

Bake the lasagne for 45 minutes or as instructed on the lasagne packet. The lasagne can be cooked and reheated; if doing so, cover with foil for the early part of cooking and remove it for the last 5 minutes.

For a luxurious finishing touch, if you really feel like pushing the boat out, drizzle the lasagne with a small amount of truffle oil and shave a little truffle on top of each portion. Sprinkle with freshly grated Parmesan cheese and serve.

PAPPARDELLE WITH ARTICHOKE & PARMESAN

Pappardelle are wide ribbon noodles cut from fresh pasta. You will need a simple hand-cranked pasta machine to make them. The procedure is not difficult and fresh pasta does taste nicer in the dishes for which it was always intended. That being said, dried pasta is not an inferior product – just a different way of dealing with the same base material.

Quag's uses fresh artichokes, but you can substitute the best-quality cooked ones you can buy bottled in olive oil – carciofi alla Romana.

'An Italian I asked about how wide pappardelle should be cut replied charmingly, "The thickness of the ribbons in a school-girl's hair."' MW

INGREDIENTS FOR 6

285g / 10oz / 2¼ cups '00' (doppo zero) Italian wheat flour or 14% high-protein Canadian flour
2 size-2 (extra-large) eggs
2 tbsp olive oil
55g / 2oz / ⅓ cup semolina flour
100ml / 3½fl oz / ½ cup extra-virgin olive oil
12 carciofi alla Romana (baby artichokes in olive oil)
2 tbsp chopped flat-leaf parsley
115g / 4oz Parmesan cheese, chopped into crumbs
black pepper

Put the flour, eggs and olive oil in a food processor and whizz briefly until the mixture crumbs. Transfer to a semolina-floured surface and press together to form a rough dough. Mound into a ball, cling-wrap and rest for 1 hour.

Cut the dough into 4 pieces and work through the pasta machine, constantly dusting with semolina flour and taking it down to sheets at no. 1 setting. Use a fluted pasta wheel to cut across the sheets to make fat noodles, say 2cm / ¾in wide. Spread out and leave for 10 minutes to dry a little. Then layer on a tray between sheets of greaseproof paper dusted with more semolina flour.

Bring a big pot of lightly salted water to a fast boil. Cook the pasta for 2 minutes in rapidly boiling water and drain in a colander, returning to the pan before all the water has evaporated.

While the pasta is cooking, put the olive oil in a frying pan over a low heat. Cut the artichokes across into slices about 1cm / ½in thick. Turn up the heat under the oil, add the artichoke slices and sauté for 30 seconds. Add to the drained pasta and toss. Add the parsley and toss again.

Serve in large warmed bowls, grind plenty of pepper over and sprinkle the Parmesan crumbs on the top.

SALADS, VEGETABLES
& MISCELLANEA

FRENCH BEAN & SESAME SALAD

The sesame dressing is Japanese in its inspiration and complements the just-cooked beans perfectly.

INGREDIENTS FOR 4

450g / 1 lb fine French green beans
85g / 3oz / 1/3 cup sesame seeds
3 tbsp sake
2 tbsp Kikkoman soy sauce
8g / 1/4oz / 1/2 tsp sugar

Top and tail the beans. Bring a large pan of salted water to the boil and blanch the beans for 3 minutes. Drain, then plunge into ice-cold water for 1 minute to stop the cooking process. Drain again and reserve. Don't leave them in the water. If you do they will lose flavour.

Put 75g / 2 1/2oz / 1/4 cup of the sesame seeds in a dry heavy frying pan over a low heat and toast, shaking from time to time, for 3 minutes until they give off a discernible aroma and are golden brown.

Bring the sake to boil in a small saucepan. It may flame briefly. Remove from the heat and leave to cool.

Put the sake, soy sauce, sugar and toasted sesame seeds in a liquidizer or processor and work to a paste. Add a tablespoon of hot water if it is too dry.

Put the beans in a bowl with the paste and toss to coat. Serve in 4 bowls, stacking the beans high and finish by sprinkling the untoasted sesame seeds on top.

QUAGLINO'S SALAD

The house salad is of Little Gem lettuce, ripe avocado and Pecorino sardo cheese in a dressing that, until now, has been kept strictly in-house. Its popularity can be judged by the fact that Quag's uses an average of 1,000 lettuces a week in its preparation. Little Gems have a nice clean-tasting leaf, but you can also use cos lettuces. Buy avocados a few days in advance and leave them to ripen at room temperature. They are ripe when the skin gives easily to light pressure, leaving an indentation.

'I developed this dressing at Café Polperro, my restaurant in Perth. Whatever new thing came in from Europe I would try to incorporate in my cooking. In this case, the inspiration was shallot vinegar.' MW

INGREDIENTS FOR 4

2 ripe avocados
3 Little Gem (Bibb) lettuces
4 long wafer-thin slices of Pecorino sardo cheese
3 tbsp extra-virgin olive oil

for the dressing:
1 garlic clove
3 tbsp shallot vinegar
1 egg, plus 2 extra egg yolks
250ml / 8 fl oz / 1 cup sunflower oil
55g / 2oz / 2/3 cup Parmesan, grated
salt and pepper

First make the dressing: peel, smash and chop the garlic finely. Put into a food processor with the vinegar, whole egg and egg yolks. Whizz until light and frothy, then add the oil in a thin stream through the feeder tube. Add the grated Parmesan, and salt and pepper to taste. Process again briefly. You should have a thin mayonnaise consistency. If too thick, drip in warm water through the feeder tube while continuing to process until you have this desired consistency.

Cut the avocados in half and remove the stones, then peel away the skins. Cut the flesh lengthwise into thin strips and reserve.

Trim off the base of the lettuces, wash the leaves and spin dry. Arrange half the leaves on 4 serving plates, then fan a half avocado on top. Put the remaining leaves on this and spoon over the dressing. Put a slice of cheese on top, dribble a little of the extra-virgin olive oil on that and finish with a few turns of black pepper.

AUBERGINE / EGGPLANT & ROAST PEPPER SALAD

Aubergines (eggplant) and red peppers happily combine in this dish, which can be served hot as a main-course accompaniment or at room temperature as a starter. It also makes a delicious topping for crostini.

'The amount of oil used in this dish is a matter of personal preference. Aubergines are like sponges and will absorb ridiculous amounts if you let them. If serving cold, then never do so straight from the fridge.' MW

INGREDIENTS FOR 6

4 red peppers
about 150ml / $^1/_4$pt / $^2/_3$ cup extra-virgin olive oil
2 medium aubergines (eggplant)
2 tbsp thyme leaves
2 garlic cloves
3 tsp balsamic vinegar
salt and pepper
crusty bread, to serve

Preheat the oven to 180°C / 350°F / gas 4.

Brush the peppers with oil, then roast them on a tray, turning once, for about 30 minutes. They should have started to collapse and soften. Remove and put into a zip-lock bag or in a bowl covered with cling-film for 10 minutes, to allow the steam to loosen the skins. Then peel, cut in half and put upside down in a sieve over a bowl to catch the juices. Reserve peppers and juices.

Peel the aubergines and cut them across into 1cm / $^1/_2$in slices. Brush these with oil and put in a non-stick pan over a high heat. Cook in batches, turning frequently and adding more oil as you go along. They should be dark golden-brown on both sides.

Scrape the seeds out of the peppers, then cut each half into 3 strips. Strip all the leaves off the thyme. Peel

Aubergine (eggplant) & roast pepper salad

the garlic and cut it into wafer-thin slices.

Choose an ovenproof dish that can be brought to the table and brush it with oil. Lay alternating slices of aubergine and pepper in rows like overlapping playing cards. Repeat to fill the dish with similar layers (usually 2). Season each layer and scatter over some of the thyme leaves and garlic. Drizzle olive oil over the top. Bake for 40 minutes, or until the top is nicely browned.

Mix the reserved pepper juices with 2 tablespoons of olive oil and the balsamic vinegar. Dress the surface with this and serve immediately or allow to cool to room temperature and serve with crusty bread.

ENDIVE, ROQUEFORT & WALNUT SALAD

Chicory is often called Belgian endive or just plain endive by the Americans and Australians. There are many diners from these countries visiting Quag's, hence the use of the name in the Quag's menu. It is a white winter vegetable that is grown in the dark in forcing beds warmed by hot pipes. The exclusion of light is essential in its production, or the leaves go green and curly. Not as curly as frisée, which is also called curly endive or chicory just to confuse us all. Here the rich salty Roquefort balances the endive's clean but slightly bitter taste to perfection. Both are complemented by the inclusion of chopped walnuts.

'Not every salad dressing demands olive oil and here is a case in point. The walnut oil would be too intense if used in isolation, so it is mixed with a neutral sunflower oil to achieve the right balance.' MW

INGREDIENTS FOR 4

150g / $5^1/_2$oz Roquefort cheese
4 heads of white endive
100g / $3^1/_2$oz / $^3/_4$ cup walnut halves
small bunch of chives

for the dressing:
1 egg yolk
1 tbsp red wine vinegar
3 tsp Dijon mustard
1 tsp salt
¹/₂ tsp pepper
1 tbsp walnut oil
300ml / ¹/₂pt / 1¹/₄ cup sunflower oil

Put the cheese in the freezer to firm up for 15 minutes. This will make it easier to crumble.

Make the dressing: in a bowl, whisk the egg yolk with the vinegar, mustard, salt and pepper. Now whisk in the walnut oil a few drops at a time, followed by the sunflower oil in a thin stream until you have a thick emulsified sauce. If it becomes too thick at any stage, thin with a few teaspoons of warm water.

Trim the bases off the endives and separate the leaves. Crumble the cheese into pieces about 1cm / ¹/₂ in and chop the walnuts to a similar size.

Toss the leaves in a bowl with the dressing to coat evenly, then build them into mounds on individual plates. Sprinkle on the cheese, followed by the walnuts and finally the chopped chives. Finish with a little coarsely ground pepper.

ENDIVE SALAD WITH MUSTARD DRESSING & CHIVES

This is less rich than the previous endive salad. The key to the success of it is lots of very good Dijon mustard in the dressing.

INGREDIENTS FOR 4
4 heads of endive
small bunch of chives

for the dressing:
1 tbsp walnut or hazelnut oil
3 tbsp sunflower, groundnut or corn oil

Rocket (arugula) & Parmesan salad

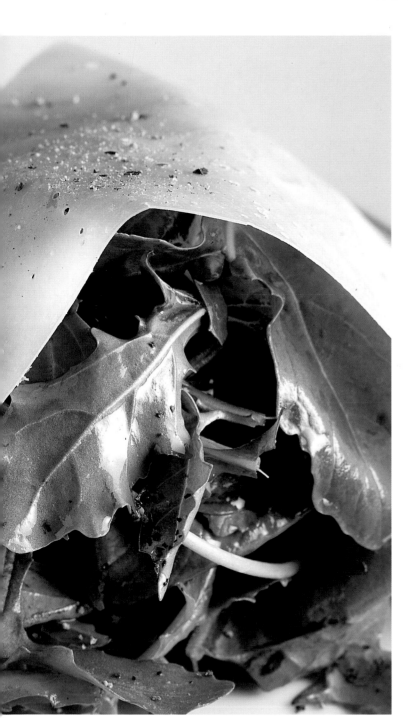

4 tbsp Dijon mustard
2 tbsp white wine vinegar
$^1/_2$ tsp salt
$^1/_4$ tsp black pepper
200ml / 7 fl oz / $^3/_4$ cup single (light) cream

Put all the dressing ingredients except the cream into a bowl and whisk hard for 3 minutes. Add the cream and stir. Hold at room temperature.

Cut off the bases of the endive and separate the leaves. Coat the leaves in the dressing, then build into pyramids on individual plates.

Scatter with chopped chives and finish with a few turns of the pepper mill.

ROCKET / ARUGULA & PARMESAN SALAD

'We actually use more than 65 kg / 143 lb of rocket (arugula) a week in our salads. A popular combination is rocket (arugula) and Parmesan, which is tossed in the house dressing.' MW

INGREDIENTS FOR 4
170g / 6oz rocket (arugula) leaves
170g / 6oz Parmesan
4 tbsp extra-virgin olive oil
black pepper

for the house dressing:
100ml / 3$^1/_2$fl oz / $^1/_2$ cup extra-virgin olive oil
2 tbsp red wine vinegar

Make the dressing by putting the ingredients into a bottle with a good grinding of black pepper.

Put the rocket in a large bowl, add the shaken dressing and toss well. Mound the leaves on 4 plates, cover the top with wafer-thin slices of Parmesan shaved with a potato peeler. Dribble a little olive oil on top and finish with some milled black pepper.

DRESSINGS

When making salad dressings, there is a tendency to fall into the habit of using the same mixture to coat everything. Here are two very different variations.

TOMATO VINAIGRETTE

INGREDIENTS FOR 8–10

450g / 1lb plum tomatoes
30g / 1oz / approx. 8 cloves garlic, finely chopped
115g / 4oz shallots, finely chopped
425ml / ³/4pt / 1²/3 cups virgin olive oil
3¹/2 tbsp champagne vinegar
55g / 2oz / ¹/4 cup tomato passata (finely chopped tomatoes)
2 tbsp basil
2 tbsp tarragon
balsamic vinegar, to taste
salt and pepper

Blanch the tomatoes in boiling water and remove the skins. Cut them in half and deseed them. Sweat the garlic and shallots in a little oil, until soft. Stir in the champagne vinegar and reduce. Add the tomatoes and passata and cook for 3 minutes. Add the herbs and remaining oil and cook for 30 minutes, over low heat, stirring occasionally. When cool, blitz in a food processor. Season with balsamic vinegar, salt and pepper.

TOMATO SALAD DRESSING

INGREDIENTS FOR 8–10

6 tbsp dark French mustard
1 tbsp sugar
150ml / ¹/4pt / ²/3 cup malt vinegar
450ml / ³/4pt / 2¹/2 cups sunflower oil
salt and pepper

Whisk the mustard, sugar and vinegar together in a bowl. Add the oil, whisking hard. Season to taste.

SIDE DISHES

QUAGLINO'S MASHED POTATOES

People rave about the restaurant's creamy-smooth mashed potatoes, though there is no secret about their success. The potatoes should be of a floury variety like a Desiré, Idaho or Russet, they should be cooked whole and allowed to dry properly before mashing with plenty of butter and a little milk.

'The best way of making mash is with an old fashioned potato masher. Any machine works the starch out of the potatoes, giving them a nasty, gluey finish.' MW

INGREDIENTS FOR 4

675g / 1¹/2lb potatoes
115g / 4oz / 1 stick unsalted butter
150ml / ¹/4pt / ¹/2 cup full fat milk
sea salt and white pepper

Peel and rinse the potatoes, then cover them in a saucepan with cold water. Salt them and bring to the boil, lowering the heat to medium. The water should be bubbling but not boiling furiously. Cook for approximately 20 minutes or until they are just cooked all the way through.

Drain the potatoes through a colander and leave for a couple of minutes to steam dry before returning to the hot pan and mashing them. Only when free of all lumps should you begin to add the butter, beating this in a piece at a time with a wooden spoon. Heat the milk and whip this in at the end. Taste and season with salt and white pepper.

Bring to the table with a small knob of butter on top.

CHIPS / FRENCH FRIES

Quaglino's cooks more than 1¹/₂ tonnes of frites a week – the thin chip introduced by the French to America and then via there to us as 'French fries'. On this scale, it would not be possible to make them so they are bought in. Real chips to go with battered fish are a different matter and are made fresh.

> *'Deep-frying at home is not easy. Domestic fryers have got better, but they can still only cook small batches. The cardinal rule is do not overcrowd the pan and always cook chips in two stages.'* MW

INGREDIENTS FOR 6

900g / 2lb floury (Idaho-type) potatoes
about 2 litres / 3¹/₂pt / 8³/₄ cups sunflower oil
salt

Peel the potatoes and cut lengthwise in 2cm / ³/₄in slices, then cut these across into chips about 1cm / ¹/₂in thick. Put into cold water for 10 minutes to remove surface starch, drain through a colander and pat dry.

Preheat the sunflower oil in an electric fryer to 190°C / 375°F. If doing so on top of the hob (stove), never deep-fry at a depth of more than half the pan and use one with a lid that can be put on in case of fire. Always gauge the temperature with a thermometer.

Blanch the chips (fries) in batches for 5 minutes, remove and reserve. Plunge them back in the basket to brown and crisp. This will take about 60 seconds. Shake the basket over the oil to drain, then empty the chips (fries) on kitchen paper.

Season with salt immediately.

TURNIP GRATIN

The humble turnip makes a sumptuous gratin that both surprises and pleases those who feel less than positive about one of our most underrated root vegetables. It is made very much like a potato gratin, but with less cream than, say, a gratin dauphinoise. Use smallish turnips that can be cut into rounds. The inclusion of mustard and spring onions gives the dish more impact.

INGREDIENTS FOR 4

900g / 2lb turnips
4 spring onions (scallions)
1 tbsp crème fraîche
4 tbsp double cream
1 tbsp Dijon mustard
55g / 2oz / 4 tbsp butter
55g / 2oz / ²/₃ cup Parmesan, grated
salt and pepper

Preheat the oven to 180°C / 350°F / gas 4 and butter a gratin dish.

Peel the turnips and slice them into rounds about 5mm / ¹/₄in thick. Blanch for 2 minutes in rapidly boiling salted water and drain. Return to a hot pan and shake to dry out excess moisture.

Trim the spring onions and cut them across into thin slices. Put into a large bowl. Add the crème fraîche, cream and mustard. Season generously with salt and pepper and whisk to mix.

Add the turnip slices and toss to coat. Then spoon into the gratin dish. Pack down to give a flat surface. Dot the top with butter, sprinkle with grated cheese and bake for 45 minutes.

ROAST TOMATOES

> *'One way to get the best out of your tomatoes is to roast them, which reduces water content and intensifies flavour. They have so many uses it is worth doing them in large batches as they can be packed in jars, covered with olive oil and kept for up to a month. This oil, and the oil and juice residue from the tins in which they are cooked, make a delicious dressing.'* MW

1 tbsp sea salt
handful of flat-leaf parsley
20 basil leaves
10 sage leaves
handful of tarragon
handful of marjoram
1.5kg / 3¹/₂lb ripe plum tomatoes
black pepper
75ml / 5 tbsp olive oil

Scatter sea salt on the base of 2 roasting tins into which the tomatoes will just fit in a single layer. Bruise the herbs and scatter half of them on the salt. Cut out the eyes of the tomatoes and slice them in half lengthwise before placing in the roasting tins, cut-side up. Salt them lightly and grind over some black pepper. Bruise the remaining herbs and arrange on top, then drizzle over the olive oil. Cover with a clean tea (dish) towel and leave overnight at room temperature.

Preheat the oven to 230°C /450°F /gas 8. Remove the tea (dish) towel and top layer of herbs, and put the trays in for 10 minutes. Then lower the temperature to 140°C / 275°F / gas 1 (with convection) or 150°C / 300°F /gas 2 (without convection) for 2 hours.

Remove and allow to cool. If not using immediately, pack in sterilised Kilner jars and fill to cover with olive oil.

STOCKS & OILS

Stocks are the life-blood of any decent kitchen. Veal stock, fond brun, is the classic base stock of French cooking. The issue of box-rearing veal has moral and ethical dimensions which are for personal agonizing and individual choice. A good chicken stock in the domestic context will, in any case, give you the base flavour you need for any meat dish. We have decided therefore not to include a veal stock recipe and suggest you use this brown chicken stock instead.

If you have roasted a chicken then you have the basis for a stock, but one carcass has obvious limitations in the amount of well-flavoured stock it can produce. Your butcher will give you carcasses if you are a regular customer. Chicken wings will also produce excellent results, once roasted to a good colour in the oven. Chicken giblets are now rarely obtainable because of EU rulings which militate against the sale of undrawn poultry. If you do have giblets, never use livers when making stock.

'The key to stock-making is long, slow simmering. The liquid is only brought to the boil initially, with the heat being lowered immediately after skimming. Boiling forces albumen from the bones and gives the stock a nasty-tasting and clouded result. Meat and poultry stocks can be simmered for several hours. You then strain them through a sieve and boil to reduce and intensify flavour. This reduction is called a jus and after further reduction may be frozen in ice-trays with the cubes bagged and kept in the freezer. You will then always have a jus ready when you need it.' MW

CHICKEN STOCK

1.8kg / 4lb raw chicken carcasses or wings
3 onions, halved but unpeeled
3 leeks, split and washed
4 celery sticks

3 carrots, peeled
1 sprig of thyme
handful of parsley
2 bay leaves
1 tbsp black peppercorns, lightly crushed

Preheat the oven to 240°C / 475°F / gas 9. Put the carcasses or chicken wings in a roasting tin and brown in the oven for 30 minutes, turning frequently.

Transfer the bones to a large pan and cover with 4.5 litres / 8pts of cold water. Bring to a boil and skim the scum from the surface. Add the vegetables and aromatics and return to the boil. Skim again, then reduce to a bare simmer and cook for a minimum of 4 hours, topping up with more water from time to time. A stock may be simmered like this overnight.

Pass through a muslin (cheesecloth)-lined sieve into a clean pan and return this to a fast boil, reducing by two-thirds. Alternatively, take the reduction further until it is syrupy and freeze as cubes.

ROAST PEPPER OIL

Every time you roast peppers for a salad or our tart (see page 84) you can get a bonus by bottling the olive oil and cooking juices to use as a delicious dressing. Use more oil than normal – say 250ml / 8fl oz / 1 cup for every 4 peppers.

8 red peppers
500ml / 17fl oz / 2 cups olive oil
salt and pepper

Preheat the oven to 220°C / 425°F / gas 7.

Put the peppers, whole, in a roasting tin. Pour over half the oil, season with salt and pepper and roast, turning frequently for about 30 minutes.

Remove from the oven and leave to cool in the tin. When you can handle them, pull out the stalks, peel the peppers and scrape out the seeds over the tin so you don't lose any of the juices.

Reserve the peppers for your salad etc. and pass the juices from the tin through a sieve into a bowl. Add the rest of the unused oil and bottle through a funnel. Refrigerate and use as fancy dictates – it is very good for dressing salads, grilled fish or red meats.

CRUSTACEA OIL

The flesh of lobsters, crabs, crayfish and prawns is highly prized, but making the most of shells, to give their strong and unique flavour to stocks, sauces and oils, makes both culinary and economic sense. Either smash shells up and freeze in bags for fish soup or use them as here to make a delicious and aromatic oil.

1 carrot
2 shallots
¼ fennel bulb
6 garlic cloves
1 celery stick
500ml / 17fl oz / 2 cups light olive oil
450g / 1lb crab, prawn (shrimp) or lobster shells or a combination
2 tbsp brandy
55g / 2oz / ⅓ cup tomatoes, chopped
55g / 2oz / ¼ cup tomato purée
1 tbsp chopped tarragon
1 tbsp chopped flat-leaf parsley
1 star anise
3 crushed peppercorns

Coarsely dice the carrot, shallots, fennel, garlic and celery.

Put 4 tablespoons of the oil in a big casserole and fry the shells over a medium heat until they go white. Add the diced vegetables and continue cooking and stirring for 5 minutes. This cooks off any meat clinging to the shells, which will otherwise go off and ruin the oil.

Add the brandy and flame it carefully, then add the chopped tomatoes and tomato purée with the herbs and

spices. Pour over the remaining oil and simmer over the lowest possible heat for 2 hours.

Strain through a sieve lined with fine muslin (cheesecloth) into a bottle via a funnel, and refrigerate. Use for dressing seafood salads or grilled fish.

MISCELLANEA

TOMATO CONCASSÉ

This is tomato which has been peeled, deseeded and cut into small dice. It is used extensively in restaurant cooking, both raw and barely cooked. The tomatoes used should be ripe, and give a sweet fresh lift to a dish.

CHEESE STRAWS

These are one of the things served in the bar with drinks. No matter how many are baked, they seem to get eaten just as quickly.

INGREDIENTS FOR 60

225g / 8oz / 2 cups plain (all-purpose) flour
225g / 8oz / 2 sticks unsalted butter
170g / 6oz farmhouse Cheddar or Parmesan,
  plus more for sprinkling
2 tsp cayenne pepper
$1/2$ tsp salt

Rub the flour, butter, cheese, cayenne pepper and salt together by hand or whizz to a crumb in a food processor. Add 1 tablespoon of water and bind. Cling-wrap and refrigerate for 1 hour.

Preheat the oven to 180°C / 350°F / gas 4 and grease 2 baking trays with a little butter.

Roll the mixture out on a lightly-floured surface to a thickness of about 5mm / $1/4$in. Cut into strips. Sprinkle with a little grated cheese, put on the tray and bake for 10 minutes. Serve while still warm.

RED PEPPER & TOMATO CHUTNEY

Bacteria, yeasts and fungi lie in wait to ruin your chutneys. Always sterilise jars before filling. Wash them in hot water with detergent, rinse well and put in a large pan. Cover completely with water, and boil for 5 minutes. Leave to cool and remove with clean hands or tongs and stand rim down on a clean cloth to dry. Lids and rubber sealing rings should be boiled too.

Once opened, keep chutney in the refrigerator.

450g / 1lb sweet red peppers
250ml / 8fl oz / 1 cup olive oil
1 tsp Maldon sea salt
1 tsp ground black pepper
900g / 2lb ripe tomatoes
350g / 12oz white onions
750ml / 1$1/4$ / 3$1/3$ cups malt vinegar
350g / 12oz / 1$1/2$ cups Thai palm
  (or light brown) sugar
2 tsp yellow mustard seeds
$3/4$ tsp allspice

Preheat the oven to 220°C / 425°F / gas 7. Put the peppers, whole, in a roasting tin. Pour over the oil, season with salt and pepper and roast, turning frequently for about 30 minutes.

Remove from the oven and leave to cool in the tin. When you can handle them, pull out the stalks, peel the peppers and scrape out the seeds. Cut the flesh into 1cm / $1/2$in dice and reserve.

Blanch the tomatoes in boiling water for 15 seconds. Refresh in cold water, peel and cut in quarters. Scrape out the seed pulp. Chop the flesh into 1cm / $1/2$in dice. Peel the onions and cut into 1cm / $1/2$in dice.

Put the vinegar, palm sugar and mustard seeds in a pan and bring to the boil. Add the peppers, tomatoes and onions, followed by the salt and spices. Lower the heat and simmer for 45 minutes.

Remove from the heat and allow to cool in the pan. When barely warm, pack into sterilized jars.

LIME & CORIANDER BUTTER

A delicious butter to top grilled fish or chicken.

115g / 4oz / 1 stick unsalted butter, diced
4 tbsp chopped coriander leaves
juice and grated zest of 1 lime
1 hot red chilli, deseeded and shredded
2 tsp Worcestershire sauce
salt

Put all the ingredients into a food processor and blitz to a paste. Taste and add a little salt if you think it needs it.

Spoon on to a sheet of cling-film and roll into a cylinder. Freeze, then cut off discs as required.

ONION CONFIT

This delicious relish goes well with pâtés and cold meats.

1kg / 2¹/₄lb onions
100g / 3¹/₂oz / 7 tbsp unsalted butter
115g / 4oz / ¹/₂ cup sugar
350ml / 12fl oz / 1¹/₂ cups red wine
3 tbsp sherry vinegar
2 tsp sea salt
1 tsp pepper

Peel the onions, then cut in half lengthwise. Place cut sides down and slice very thinly from top to bottom.

Melt the butter over a low heat, then add the onions. Stir to coat, and sweat gently until collapsed, stirring frequently. Increase the heat to medium and, stirring constantly, take the onions to a golden brown.

As they start to darken further, add the sugar, red wine, sherry vinegar, salt and pepper. Reduce the heat and continue to cook slowly, stirring until most of the liquid has evaporated and you are left with a moist, jammy residue. Remove from the heat, stir and leave to cool.

Pack into jars and keep in the fridge.

WELSH RAREBIT

A great lunch or supper dish followed by a salad. The key is not to overcook the cheese. Apply too much heat or cook for too long and fat will separate out, making the finished result oily.

'Larger amounts can be made and refrigerated and served in smaller portions as a savoury to end a meal. A marvellous dish with which to finish drinking your red wine.' MW

INGREDIENTS FOR 4

55g / 2oz / 4 tbsp butter
55g / 2oz / ¹/₂ cup flour
250ml / 8fl oz / 1 cup milk
5 tbsp beer (real ale, not lager)
15g / ¹/₂oz / 6 tbsp English mustard
3 tsp Worcestershire sauce
350g / 12oz farmhouse Cheddar, grated
4 slices of decent white bread
salt and pepper

Melt the butter in a pan, then stir in the flour to make a thick roux. Beat in the milk, followed by the beer. When amalgamated, add the mustard, Worcestershire sauce and 1 teaspoon of pepper, followed finally by the grated cheese.

Cook, stirring over a low heat just to the point where the cheese has melted and you have a nice smooth elastic mixture, which will take 3–5 minutes.

Use on toast immediately (see below), or pour and spoon into a shallow Swiss-roll tin and leave to set. This can be refrigerated for 2–3 days.

When you want to eat your rarebit, preheat a medium grill (broiler) and cut the crusts off the bread. Toast under the grill (broiler).

Cut pieces of rarebit from the tray to a size slightly smaller than the pieces of bread, and lay on top. Put back under the grill (broiler) until bubbling hot and golden brown and serve at once.

DESSERTS

142–143

PAVLOVA WITH BERRIES

A spectacularly pretty dessert, full of colour and flavour. The textures of the meringue, crisp without and marshmallow soft at the centre, contrast perfectly with the succulent berry coulis and the thick rich cream.

'Without doubt our most popular dessert and one that brings summer to the table all year round. The inclusion of the boiling water and the vinegar are important in achieving the right contrast between the exterior of the meringue and the centre. Ovens at low temperatures can be temperamental, hence the variable cooking time.' MW

INGREDIENTS FOR 4
225g / 8oz punnet of strawberries
225g / 8oz punnet of raspberries
225g / 8oz punnet of blueberries
225g / 8oz punnet of blackberries
200g / 7oz / ³/₄ cup sugar
250ml / 8fl oz / 1 cup double (heavy) cream
3 tbsp thick plain yoghurt

for the meringue:
whites of 6 eggs
200g / 7oz / ³/₄ cup sugar
1 tsp vanilla essence
1 tsp white wine or champagne vinegar
¹/₂ tbsp boiling water

Preheat the oven to 140°C / 275°F / gas 1.

To make the meringue: whisk all the ingredients together for 5–10 minutes. With a large spoon, spread the meringue mixture in 4 mounded circles on a silicone baking sheet or greaseproof paper on a baking sheet. Since they are not being dried out, they will not have the same tendency to stick as do crisp meringues.

Bake for 45–60 minutes. The pavlovas should be crisp, but only lightly tinted on the outside and soft marshmallow in the centre.

Reserve, whole, a few perfect specimens of each berry. Put the rest in a pan with the sugar, bring to the boil and liquidize. Pass through a sieve and cool. Stir in the whole berries.

Whisk the cream and yoghurt together until thick enough to scoop.

To serve, top with a spoonful of the cream, finishing off with the fresh berries and the coulis, allowing some to overflow.

Pavlova with berries

RICE PUDDING WITH PLUM COMPOTE

The thin and milky pudding of childhood is not a pleasant memory. Enrich it with a little cream and condensed milk and you have a silky smooth dessert to grace the finest table.

'Do not be surprised by the small amount of rice: 55g / 2oz / ¹/₄ cup per 575ml / 1pt / 2¹/₂ cups is ideal. A fruit compote is just the thing to go with a sweet and rich pudding. It should not be too sweet, so as to provide contrast.' MW

INGREDIENTS FOR 4

55g / 2oz / ¹/₄ cup pudding (short-grain) rice
30g / 1oz / 2 tbsp unsalted butter
1 tsp sugar
575ml / 1pt / 2¹/₂ cups full-fat milk
2 tbsp double (heavy) cream
2 tbsp condensed milk
1 pinch of salt

for the plum compote:
6 large plums
2 tbsp sugar
zest of 1 lemon

Put all the rice pudding ingredients together in a saucepan. Slowly, bring to the boil, lower the heat to a bare simmer and cook gently for about 30 minutes. While cooking, stir well from the bottom of the pan at regular intervals with a small wooden spoon, taking care to push down to the sides where it will otherwise stick and burn.

For the compote: slice the plums thinly into quarters, discarding the stones, and put in a pan together with the sugar and lemon zest. Cook the compote gently over a medium heat until soft.

Serve the rice pudding with the plum compote on the side.

Rice pudding with plum compote

WHITE CHOCOLATE TORTE WITH RASPBERRIES

True chocolate contains a minimum of 34% cocoa solids, made up of cocoa mass and cocoa butter. White chocolate, in contrast, has had the former removed and does not therefore have the same rich intensity as dark chocolate.

'Seek out a premium brand like Lindt, as cheaper white chocolate substitutes vegetable oil for cocoa butter and tends to cake when melted. All ingredients should be at room temperature before you start.' MW.

INGREDIENTS FOR 6

24cm / 9¹/₂ in ready-made sponge cake base
6 tbsp Cointreau
350g / 12oz white chocolate
750ml / 1¹/₄pt / 3¹/₈ cups double (heavy) cream
icing (confectioners') sugar, to dust
225g / 8oz punnet of fresh raspberries

Put the sponge into a spring-form tin and spoon over half the Cointreau.

Melt all but 55g / 2oz of the chocolate by breaking it into small pieces and putting it in a glass bowl set over, but not touching, hot water. The water should not be boiling. Put the remaining chocolate in the fridge until ready to serve.

Heat to the point where the chocolate melts, stirring from time to time with a metal spoon.

Whisk the cream to soft peaks and fold into the chocolate mixture. At the same time, add the Cointreau, then pour the mixture over the sponge base and refrigerate overnight.

Before serving, top with flakes of the reserved white chocolate (use a potato peeler to make the shavings), dust with icing sugar and cut into portions with a warm knife.

Serve with fresh raspberries.

PASSION FRUIT TART

Different fruits give new spins to old themes. Passion fruits are the smaller, juicier relatives of pomegranates. When cooking it is important not to take the custard too far. It should be set, but still wobble slightly when it comes from the oven.

> *'In Australia fresh passion fruit are cheap. Here it is more economical to use frozen passion pulp but this also means increasing the amount of sugar to compensate for its sourness.'* MW

Passion fruit tart

INGREDIENTS FOR 6

25cm / 10in sweet shortcrust pastry shell, baked blind (see page 156)
175ml / 6fl oz / $^3/_4$ cup passion fruit pulp
200g / 7oz / $^3/_4$ cup sugar
5 eggs
200ml / 7fl oz / $^7/_8$ cup double (heavy) cream
150ml / $^1/_4$pt / $^2/_3$ cup whipping cream
3 fresh passion fruit

Preheat the oven to 180°C / 350°F / gas 4 and stand the tart shell on a baking tray.

Whisk the fruit pulp and sugar together. In another bowl whisk the eggs, adding the double cream until combined. Gently whisk this mixture into the sweetened fruit pulp, then pass through a fine sieve and pour this custard into the tart shell.

Bake for 35–40 minutes. Press the surface gently to check it is set, returning for another 5 minutes if it is still too liquid. It should wobble slightly, resembling a set jelly.

Whisk the whipping cream to soft peaks.

When the tart has cooled, cut it into 6 pieces. Put a spoonful of cream beside each portion. Cut the passion fruit in half and spoon the pulp on top of the cream.

HOT PARKIN PUDDING & CUSTARD

This has all the ingredients that make a great British pudding: sticky treacle and sugar, eggs, butter and spice. Originally served cold as a cross between a biscuit and a cake, this version is more moist and served hot with either crème Anglaise or butterscotch sauce, or both.

INGREDIENTS FOR 6

115 g / 4 oz / 1 cup plain (all-purpose) flour
pinch of salt
1 tsp ground ginger
1/4 tsp ground cinnamon
1/4 tsp ground cloves
1/4 tsp bicarbonate of (baking) soda
1/4 tsp baking powder
115 g / 4 oz / 1 cup pinhead (finely ground) oatmeal
75 g / 2 1/2 oz / 1/3 cup soft dark brown sugar
75 g / 2 1/2 oz / 5 tbsp unsalted butter
75 g / 2 1/2 oz / 1/3 cup black treacle (molasses)
75 g / 2 1/2 oz / 1/3 cup golden (light corn) syrup
3 eggs
butter, for greasing
crème Anglaise (see page 157), to serve
butterscotch sauce (see page 157), to serve

Preheat the oven to 180°C / 350°F / gas 4. Butter a 33 cm / 9 in square cake tin and line the base with greaseproof paper.

Sift the flour, salt, ginger, cinnamon, cloves, bicarbonate of soda and baking powder into a bowl. Add the oatmeal and reserve.

Put the sugar, butter, treacle and syrup in a pan and melt over a low heat until the sugar has dissolved.

Then, off the heat, beat the eggs in one at a time. Add to the flour mixture and stir to a smooth batter.

Pour into the prepared square cake tin and bake for 50–60 minutes.

When cooked, remove from the tin and cut into squares. Place a little crème Anglaise on each plate, top with a square of parkin and spoon over some of the butterscotch sauce.

PEAR & HONEY TART

INGREDIENTS FOR 6

8 ripe pears
1 bottle of white wine
200 g / 7 oz / 3/4 cup sugar
1 cinnamon stick
juice and pared zest of 1 lemon
juice and pared zest of 1 orange
25 cm / 10 in sweet shortcrust pastry shell, baked blind (see page 156)

for the custard:

4 eggs
450 ml / 3/4 pt / 1 7/8 cups double (heavy) cream
120 ml / 4 fl oz / 1/2 cup Poire William
170 g / 6 oz / 3/4 cup ground almonds
115 g / 4 oz / 1/2 cup clear honey

Preheat the oven to 220°C / 425°F / gas 7.

Peel, halve and core the pears. Place in a pan with the wine, sugar, cinnamon, and citrus zest and juice. Bring to the boil. Immediately remove from the heat and leave to cool. Remove the pears to drain.

Make the custard: whisk the eggs and the cream together. Whisk in the Poire William, then the ground almonds and finally the honey.

Put the tart shell on a baking tray. Lay the pears, cut surfaces down and pointing inwards, on the base of the tart and pour the custard over.

Bake until brown on the surface and just set. This should take about 15 minutes. Remove and let cool. Serve at room temperature.

Sauternes custard with Armagnac prunes

SAUTERNES CUSTARD WITH ARMAGNAC PRUNES

The British are loathe to eat any dish which they are told features prunes. Would they be happier if they were called dried plums? Those who overcome their prejudice and taste them with this sublime custard are invariably converted. While the recipe specifies Agen prunes, the most superior French prunes that are used in the restaurant, there are now very good pitted California prunes that will be fine. The Armagnac used to flavour the prunes has a unique flavour, but you could use brandy. The custard is best made the day before.

'I was introduced to this custard by Philip Searle, the owner/chef of Oasis Seros in Sydney.' MW

INGREDIENTS FOR 6
115g / 4oz / $^1/_2$ cup sugar
3 eggs, plus 9 extra egg yolks
150g / 5$^1/_2$oz / $^3/_4$ cup vanilla sugar
700ml / 1$^1/_4$pt / 3$^1/_3$ cups whipping cream
375ml / 13fl oz / 1$^2/_3$ cup Sauternes or other dessert wine
butter, for greasing

for the prunes:
2 tea bags
225g / 8oz / 1 cup pitted prunes
115g / 4oz / $^1/_2$ cup sugar
1 cinnamon stick
3 strips of orange peel
2 strips of lemon peel
150ml / $^1/_4$pt / $^2/_3$ cup Armagnac

At least a week before and up to a month in advance, prepare the prunes: make 575ml / 1pt / 2$^1/_2$ cups of tea with the tea bags. Leave for 2 minutes, then discard the bags and pour the weak tea into a saucepan.

Add the prunes, sugar, cinnamon stick and citrus

peels. Bring to the boil, lower the heat and simmer gently for 5 minutes. Remove from the heat and leave to cool. When cold, add the Armagnac and transfer to a Kilner jar or lidded container.

On the day before serving: preheat the oven to 150°C / 300°F / gas 2. Have ready 6 buttered dariole moulds (small custard cups) and a bain-marie in which they will all stand without touching.

Put the sugar in a saucepan with 5 tablespoons of water, bring to the boil, lower the heat and bubble to a rich caramel. Pour into the base of the moulds.

Make the custard by whisking the eggs, extra yolks and vanilla sugar together. In 2 separate pans, bring the cream and the wine to a simmer. Whisk the hot wine into the eggs, followed by the cream. Pass through a fine sieve into a jug.

Pour into the moulds and put into the bain-marie. Fill with hot water to halfway up the moulds and put to bake for 45 minutes.

Remove, cool and refrigerate overnight.

To serve, dip the moulds briefly into very hot water, then run a blade round the inside. Tilt and slide out on plates. Serve with some prunes and with a little of their juice spooned over the top.

APRICOT CHEESECAKE

Some people are surprised to eat a cheesecake that does not have a biscuit base. Instead, the rich cheese and cream mixture is served en cocotte *with an apricot compote. Leftover compote is good at breakfast-time.*

INGREDIENTS FOR 6
   225g / 8oz cream cheese
   875g / 3oz / ¹/₃ cup sugar, plus more for dusting
   2 eggs, separated
   225g / 8oz / 1 cup sour cream
   butter, for greasing
   icing sugar, for dusting

for the apricot compote:
   170g / 6oz / ³/₄ cup dried apricots
   85g / 3oz / ¹/₃ cup sugar

Preheat the oven to 140°C / 275°F / gas 1. Butter 6 ramekins about 10cm / 4in wide and 3.5cm / 1¹/₂in deep and prepare a bain-marie big enough to hold them side by side.

Make the apricot compote: put the apricots, sugar and 100ml / 3¹/₂fl oz / ¹/₂ cup water in a pan. Bring to the boil, lower the heat and simmer until the apricots start to break down. Add more water if it gets too dry.

In a bowl, cream the cheese and two-thirds of the sugar together, then beat in the egg yolks. Finally, fold in the sour cream.

Whisk the egg whites, adding the remaining sugar as they start to form soft peaks. Put a spoonful into the cheese mixture and stir in before folding in the rest.

Put 1 tablespoon of compote into each ramekin and then fill with the cheese mixture to within 1cm / ¹/₂in of the top and place in the bain-marie. Fill the bain-marie with warm water to halfway up the ramekins. Bake for 25 minutes. Allow to cool completely.

Dust the tops with icing sugar before serving.

CHOCOLATE PEAR TART

The combination of chocolate, almonds and pears is classic and very good. You want a pear like a Comice, ripe but still firm. If this is difficult to find, then in the domestic context good-quality tinned pears could be substituted. However, freshly poached pears are by far the better option.

'Make sure your eggs are at room temperature. If they are cold you won't get the same rise in the frangipane. When adding the ground almonds, flour and eggs to the buttercream, do so alternately, a little of each at a time. This way your frangipane will never separate.' MW

INGREDIENTS FOR 6

6 pears
1 lemon
1 orange
225g/ 8oz / 1 cup sugar
1 cinnamon stick
575ml / 1pt / 2^1/$_2$ cups white wine
575ml / 1pt / 2^1/$_2$ cups water

for the chocolate frangipane:
115g / 4oz / 1 stick butter
3 eggs
225g / 8oz best dark chocolate
115g / 4oz / ^{1}/$_2$ cup sugar
115g / 4oz / 1^1/$_2$ cups ground almonds
30g / 1oz / ^{1}/$_4$ cup plain (all-purpose) flour
25cm / 10in sweet shortcrust pastry shell, baked
  blind (see page 156)
1 tbsp flaked almonds
icing sugar, for dusting

Peel the pears and put into a saucepan with all the other ingredients and bring to the boil. Lower the heat and poach for about 20 minutes until cooked all the way through, but not soft. Leave the pears to cool in the liquid. If using tinned pears, drain thoroughly.

Preheat the oven to 150°C / 300°F / gas 2.

Remove butter from the fridge and allow to soften at room temperature. Also make sure the eggs are at room temperature. Break the chocolate into pieces and melt in a bowl over hot water. Beat the butter and sugar until white and creamy. Beat the eggs into this mixture, adding a little at a time and interspersing with the almonds and flour. If you add all the eggs in one go you risk splitting the mixture. Finally, beat in the chocolate.

Spoon half the frangipane into the tart shell. Cut the pears in half and arrange on top, thinner ends pointing inwards. Spoon over the rest of the frangipane and sprinkle the top with flaked almonds. Bake for 1 hour.

Serve while still warm, dusting with icing sugar before bringing to the table.

Chocolate pear tart and Vanilla bean ice-cream

VANILLA BEAN ICE-CREAM

A classic vanilla ice-cream, heavily scented with vanilla pods, will always be one of the finest elements in a dessert and is, of course, the base for many flavoured ice-creams.

This version is distinguished by using several whole vanilla pods which may be rinsed, dried and used several times. Store them in a jar of caster sugar to infuse it with their heady scent and use this sugar for the next batch of ice-cream (with 4 fresh vanilla pods).

'Fresh ice-cream, although frozen, does deteriorate in flavour if left in the freezer for too long. It is best eaten the next day. The idea of adding semi-whipped cream comes from a friend of mine, Perth chef Andrew Peaston.' MW

INGREDIENTS FOR 6
500ml/ 17fl oz / 2 cups full-fat milk
6 vanilla pods
240g/ 8¹/₂oz / 1 cup sugar
9 egg yolks
**300ml/ ¹/₂pt / 1¹/₄ cups whipping cream,
 semi-whipped**

Put the milk and vanilla pods in a pan and slowly bring to the boil. While this is heating, whisk the sugar and egg yolks in a stainless-steel bowl until almost white. As soon as it boils, pour the scalded milk onto the yolks, whisking until incorporated.

Place the bowl on top of a pan of boiling water and stir constantly with a wooden spoon until the custard starts to thicken and coat the back of the spoon. Remove immediately from the heat and strain through a fine sieve into a clean bowl.

Leave the custard to cool before folding in the semi-whipped cream. Pour into an ice-cream maker and churn until frozen. Spoon into a plastic container with a lid and put in the freezer, removing 3–4 minutes before serving.

APPLE CHARLOTTE WITH CALVADOS CRÈME ANGLAISE

Sliced white loaves were obviously made with joyous things like bread and butter pudding and apple charlotte in mind. This is as good as it gets: flavoured with Calvados and served with a light brandied custard.

'While I lived in Australia, one of the things I missed most was the Bramley, the best cooking apple in the world. I have always been amazed that people like the French, who should know better, don't have an equivalent to the English Bramley. Their loss, our gain.' MW

INGREDIENTS FOR 6
10 Bramley (cooking) apples (about 1kg / 2¹/₄lb)
115g / 4oz / ¹/₂ cup sugar
100g / 3¹/₂oz / ¹/₂ cup sultanas
100ml / 3¹/₂fl oz / ¹/₂ cup Calvados
150g / 5¹/₂oz / 1 stick + 3 tbsp butter
1 sliced white loaf

for the Calvados Crème Anglaise:
**575ml / 1pt / 2¹/₂ cups Crème Anglaise
(see page 157)**
5–6 tbsp Calvados

Preheat the oven to 200°C / 400°F / gas 6.

Peel, core and dice the apples. Put in a saucepan with the sugar. Bring to the boil, turn down the heat and cook until the apples start to purée, about 10–15 minutes. Stir in the sultanas and Calvados and leave to cool.

Make the crème Anglaise as described on page 157. When cool, stir in the Calvados and reserve.

Melt the butter over a low heat. Brush a suitable pie dish or mould with the butter. Cut the crusts off the bread, dip in the butter and use to line the dish. Fill with the apple mixture and put on a lid of more bread slices dipped in butter. Bake for 30 minutes, or until the bread is golden. Serve with Calvados crème Anglaise.

ICED PRUNE & ARMAGNAC PARFAIT

The prunes in this dish are cooked with sugar to a preserve consistency, before being macerated in Armagnac. You could also use brandy or rum to ring the flavour changes. You can make the Victoria sponge (sponge cake) or buy a ready-made sponge base if you are in a hurry, since it is soaked with the alcohol and prune syrup. Buy the ready-stoned California prunes that need no prior soaking.

'When cutting this parfait into slices straight from the freezer, first dip your knife into boiling water.' MW

INGREDIENTS FOR 4
6 egg yolks
140g / 5oz / ²/₃ cup sugar
4 tbsp water
450ml / ³/₄pt / 1²/₃ cups double (heavy) cream
5 tbsp Armagnac
**20cm / 8in Victoria sponge (sponge cake), about
5cm / 2in thick**

for the prune conserve:
450g / 1lb / 2 cups pitted prunes
125g / 4¹/₂oz / ¹/₂ cup sugar
100ml / 3¹/₂fl oz / ¹/₂ cup Armagnac

First make the prune conserve: coarsely chop the prunes and put them in a pan with the sugar and 250ml / 8fl oz / 1 cup cold water. Bring to the boil, lower the heat and simmer gently until you have a liquid jam-like consistency. Allow to cool until just warm, then add the Armagnac, stir in and reserve.

Whisk the egg yolks in a bowl and reserve.

In a pan, heat the sugar and water to the soft ball stage, that is 112°C / 237°F. Starting with tiny drips, whisk this into the egg yolks until combined. Leave to cool.

Whip the cream to soft peaks, whisking in the Armagnac gradually, as it starts to thicken.

When the egg and sugar mixture is cold, fold it into the cream.

Slice the sponge horizontally into two thin layers. In a terrine, place a sheet of the sponge (you can freeze the rest for future use) and soak this sponge base with the prune syrup from the top of the prune mixture. Then top with half the prune conserve, spreading to make an even layer and top with the egg-cream mixture. Bang the terrine to get rid of any air pockets and freeze overnight.

Remove from the freezer 2 minutes before serving. Cut into portions with a hot knife and serve with a little of the remaining prune conserve on the side.

Iced prune & Armagnac parfait

CARAMEL ICE-CREAM

This ice-cream is made by the simplest method of all, incorporating a light sabayon into a rich caramel syrup, then folding in lashings of Jersey cream or the best double (heavy) cream you can lay your hands on.

'In these cholesterol-conscious times, the amount of cream and eggs used may be shocking, but in a dessert like this you taste precisely what you put into it. If you have eaten our caramel ice-cream and marvelled at how good it tastes, now you know why.' MW

INGREDIENTS FOR 8
450g / 1 lb / 2½ cups sugar
575 ml / 1pt / 2½ cups cold water
8 egg yolks
1.1 litres / 2 pt / 5 cups Jersey or best-quality
    double (heavy) cream
2 tbsp brown sugar

Put the sugar and 120ml / 4fl oz / ½ cup cold water in a pan and bring it slowly to 180°C / 350°F, when you will have a dark, seething dangerous caramel.

Remove from the heat and gradually add 250ml / 8fl oz / 1 cup cold water. The cold water coming in contact with the red-hot sugar produces a spectacular reaction, so do be very careful.

When you have added the water, return to the heat and bring back to the boil. Add the remaining 250ml / 8fl oz / 1 cup of water, return to the boil, remove and cool and reserve. Allow to cool for 5 minutes, while you whisk the egg yolks to a light white sabayon.

Continuing to whisk, pour in the caramel syrup in a thin stream until fully incorporated. Whisk until cool.

Lightly whip the cream to soft peaks, then fold into the caramel custard. Mix completely, so no streaks of cream are visible. Pour into a plastic container, put on a lid, and then freeze overnight, removing to soften for a minute before serving. Scatter over the sugar and brulée with a blow torch and serve.

Poached pears

POACHED PEARS & CINNAMON ICE-CREAM

For once this is a recipe that demands slightly under-ripe pears and there is never a problem getting hold of those.

A light and inexpensive red wine is best for the poaching. If you were wondering what to do with that bottle of Beaujolais nouveau, here is its perfect fate.

The cinnamon ice-cream needs churning in a machine; and all the preparation should be done the day before.

INGREDIENTS FOR 6

6 firm pears
1 litre / 1³/₄pt / 4¹/₃ cups red wine (see above)
225g / 8oz / 1 cup sugar
1 cinnamon stick

for the ice-cream:
500ml / 17 fl oz / 2 cups full-fat milk
6 cinnamon sticks
9 egg yolks
225g / 8oz / 1 cup sugar
1 tsp ground cinnamon
300ml / ¹/₂pt / 1¹/₄ cups whipping cream

Peel the pears, leaving the stems on. Put in a pan with the wine, sugar and cinnamon stick. Bring to the boil, turn down to a simmer and put a plate or a small lid on top to keep them beneath the surface. Poach gently for 40–45 minutes, then let cool in the liquid.

When cold, remove the pears and return the poaching liquor to a fast boil to reduce by half. Allow this syrup to cool, then return the pears to it. Coat with the syrup and leave to soak overnight.

Make the ice-cream: bring water to simmer in a saucepan in which you can place a bowl for cooking the custard.

Put the milk and cinnamon sticks in a pan and bring to the boil slowly over a low heat.

Whisk the egg yolks and sugar together in a metal or glass bowl until pale and ribboned. Remove the cinnamon sticks and pour the scalded milk into this mixture, whisking to incorporate.

Place the bowl over the simmering water and stir continuously with a wooden spoon until you have a custard thick enough to coat the back of the spoon. Add the ground cinnamon, pass through a sieve into a bowl and leave to cool to room temperature.

Whip the cream just to the point where it starts to thicken, then fold it into the custard. (Be careful not to over-churn or it will turn into butter.)

Pour and scrape into the ice-cream maker and churn until just set. Transfer to a plastic box with a lid and freeze overnight. Remove the ice-cream from the freezer 3–5 minutes before serving.

Cut the base of each pear to give a flat surface and stand upright on the plate with a neatly rolled scoop of ice-cream beside it. Spoon a little of the wine syrup over the pear.

CHOCOLATE TART

Simple yet seductively rich and dark, this tart's combination of warm chocolate filling and sweet crisp pastry is strikingly different. The better the bitter chocolate, the better the tart.

'This recipe comes from Andrew Smith, the pastry chef at Quaglino's.' MW

INGREDIENTS FOR 6

200g / 7oz dark chocolate
125g / 4¹/₂oz / 1 stick + 1 tbsp unsalted butter
1 egg, plus 3 extra egg yolks
40g / 1¹/₄oz / 4 tbsp sugar
25cm / 10in sweet shortcrust pastry shell, baked blind (see page 156)
icing (confectioners') sugar, to dust
thick pouring (heavy) cream, to serve

DESSERTS

Break the chocolate into uniform pieces and put with the butter in a bowl over a pan of just-simmering water. The bowl should not touch the water. Stir from time to time with a metal spoon until it has just melted into a homogenous mass.

Preheat the oven to 180°C / 350°F / gas 4.

Cream the eggs and sugar in the bowl of a food mixer with the whisk attachment, until light and fluffy. Add the chocolate butter mixture to the creamed eggs and sugar, and fold through gently.

Put the tart shell on a baking tray and fill with the mixture. Bake for 20 minutes.

Allow to cool, dust with icing sugar and serve at room temperature with thick pouring cream.

PASTRY

For most of us the kitchen is not a laboratory, nor is cooking a science. However, a moment's thought will remind us that when we apply heat we create chemical reactions. The success we achieve when doing so will depend, as in laboratory experiments, on the amounts of the different elements used and the temperature applied. In the making of pastry, precision is essential. It does not lend itself to slapdash modification.

'The first rule of baking is to have an accurate set of scales and always use them. The second is to work in as cool and spacious a place as possible. A marble surface for rolling is ideal if not actually essential.' MW

SHORTCRUST PASTRY

170g / 6oz / 1¹/₂ sticks butter
250g / 8¹/₂oz / 2¹/₈ cups flour
1 egg
¹/₄ tsp salt
1 tbsp milk

Dice the butter and leave to soften at room temperature for 30 minutes.

Sift the flour on to a work surface and make a well in the centre. Put the butter dice in the well, break in the egg, and add the salt. Use your fingertips to rub these in, pulling in more flour from the outside as you work.

When all has been combined, moisten with the milk and knead with the heel of your hand, making 3 turns. You should end up with a silky smooth ball of dough.

Wrap in cling-film and rest in the fridge for at least 1 hour before using.

This dough will keep in the fridge for a week and also freezes well.

SWEET SHORTCRUST PASTRY

170g / 6oz / 1¹/₂ sticks butter
300g / 10¹/₂oz / 2²/₃ cups flour
100g / 3¹/₂oz / ¹/₂ cup sugar
2 eggs
zest of 1 lemon

Follow the same procedure as above, but rub in the butter and sugar before adding the eggs. Add the lemon zest when you gather the dough together.

MAKING TART SHELLS AND BAKING BLIND

Many recipes require a ready-baked tart shell. Whether using plain (unsweetened) or sweet shortcrust pastry, the procedure is the same.

Roll the pastry out to a round about 5cm / 2in larger than the top of the tart tin. Pick the pastry up over the rolling pin and lay over the tin. Gently lift and ease it down around the sides to fit, taking care not to leave any air between the pastry and the tin.

Fold the overhanging pastry back over to give a double thickness around the edges. Squeeze this between finger and thumb to amalgamate, making sure that the top of the pastry is above the height of the sides of the tin as it will shrink during cooking.

Line the shell with a sheet of foil or greaseproof paper and fill with about 450g / 1lb of dried beans. Bake in an oven preheated to 200°C / 400°F / gas 6 for 10 minutes.

Remove the beans and the foil and return to the oven for a further 3–5 minutes to finish cooking to a uniform pale golden-brown.

BUTTERSCOTCH SAUCE

Butter, sugar and cream: simple, rich and sensational. This is one of the easiest hot sweet sauces to make, but one that never fails to please.

225g / 8oz / 1 cup sugar
100ml / 3¹/₂fl oz / ¹/₂ cup cold water
100g / 3¹/₂oz / 7 tbsp unsalted butter, diced
300ml / ¹/₂pt / 1¹/₄ cups single (light) cream

Put the sugar and cold water into a small thick-bottomed or non-stick saucepan and bring to a boil.

Lower the heat and take to 180°C / 350°F, when the caramel will have coloured from a light blond colour to dark golden-brown.

Remove the saucepan from the heat and gradually add the cream a spoonful at a time as the mixture will rise dangerously as soon as the cold cream hits the volcanic toffee.

When all the cream has been amalgamated, remove it from the heat and whisk in the diced butter until incorporated into a smooth creamy sauce. Return to the boil briefly and remove from the heat.

Use at once or allow to cool before refrigerating. It will keep in the fridge for up to a week. If reheating, do so gently, gradually returning to a boil.

CRÈME ANGLAISE

One of the few sauces of classic cuisine to be graced in French with English attribution, Crème Anglaise is the essential custard of the pastry section. It is a long way removed from the custard you make from packets or pour from tins, but is very easy to make.

'Always split the vanilla pods to expose the seeds to the milk for maximum flavour. Once rinsed and dried, store the used pods in sugar to make vanilla sugar.' MW

MAKES ABOUT 575 ML / 1 PT / 2¹/₂ CUPS
500ml / 17fl oz / 2 cups full-fat milk
2 vanilla pods, split
8 egg yolks
100g / 3¹/₂oz / ¹/₂ cup sugar

Put the milk in a pan and add the split vanilla pods and seeds. Bring slowly to the boil.

Whisk the egg yolks and sugar to a pale ribbon consistency. Slowly whisk in the milk and return to a clean saucepan. Simmer, stirring constantly, until the sauce thickens to a custard.

Then pass through a fine sieve into a bowl and cool.

CHOCOLATE SAUCE

225g / 8oz best bitter chocolate
55g / 2oz / 1¹/₄ cups sugar
100ml / 3¹/₂fl oz / ¹/₂ cup single (light) cream

Break the chocolate into pieces and put in a pan with the 350ml / 12fl oz / 1¹/₂ cups water and the sugar over a medium heat and bring to the boil, stirring all the time. The instant the first bubbles come to the surface, lower the heat and simmer gently for 15 minutes.

Stir in the cream and pass through a fine sieve. This can be served hot or cold.

INDEX

Acknowledgements

I would like to thank all the staff at Quaglino's, who made me welcome
long before this book was ever dreamed of. **RW**

I would like to thank the following chefs for all their hard work, and for
their continuous effort in maintaining the quality and standard of food that
Quaglino's has come to represent; Richard Whittington, for a most enjoyable
collaboration; and all those whose unselfish help has contributed to this book.
Sincere thanks to: John Torode, Paul Wilson, Stuart Lyall, Andrew Smith,
Richard Lee and Paul Catterson. Not forgetting four West Australians who have
since returned down under: Mark Rogers, Serina Wells, David Danks
and David McDermott. **MW**